Columbines

Columbines

Aquilegia, Paraquilegia, and *Semiaquilegia*

by Robert Nold

Timber Press
Portland · Cambridge

Photographs and illustrations are by Cindy Nelson-Nold unless otherwise noted.

Published in 2003 by
Timber Press, Inc.
The Haseltine Building
133 S.W. Second Avenue, Suite 450
Portland, Oregon 97204 U.S.A.

Timber Press
2 Station Road
Swavesey
Cambridge CB4 5QJ, U.K.

Printed in China

Library of Congress Cataloging-in-Publication Data

Nold, Robert.
    Columbines : aquilegia, paraquilegia, and semiaquilegia / by Robert Nold.
        p.   cm.
    Includes bibliographical references (p.   ).
    ISBN 0-88192-588-8
    1. Columbines. I. Title.

SB413.C634 N65 2003
635.9'3334—dc21

2002040929

For Elizabeth

Contents

Plates follow pages 80 and 112

Preface

◦⟋

"What race has so delicate and desirable a charm as this?"
—Reginald Farrer, *The English Rock-Garden*, 1919

T HE COLUMBINE—few flowers are less in need of an introduction, and
few more redolent of the essence of gardening, with its concomitant
images of continuity, concupiscence, and demise. Gardeners have cultivated columbines for hundreds of years, and will no doubt continue to do
so for centuries more. Columbines are notorious for interbreeding; they
have stood as symbols of cuckoldry and lust for ages, functioning as aphrodisiacs in the minds of people who never heard of Ophelia. Columbines, as a rule, do not live forever, nor do gardeners; but it is gardeners
who, in the peculiar pursuit of their passions, have caused certain columbines to live very close to something like forever.

The taxonomy of the genus *Aquilegia* is, to be frank, impenetrable;
each succeeding treatment seems to contradict the last. Just when we
thought the concept of a species had been clearly defined, our understanding is shifted slightly out of focus by a new treatment. John Gerard's
comment, in his famous *Herball* of 1597, that "to distinguish severally
were to small purpose, being things so familiarly known to all," seems to
presage modern frustrated contemplation of the genus as a whole.

This book takes on the whole genus but not with comprehension.
My aim is synthesis, a collocation of descriptions and opinions, wherever
I can find them. In truth, the species differ less among themselves than do

9

the selections made by gardeners, so, in a way, this book is a paean to the perseverance and continued observation that characterizes what Claude Barr (1983) called "this best of all hobbies," gardening.

Acknowledgments

⁓

EMBARKING on a book such as this one is a certain guarantee that one's own limited knowledge will be immediately and publicly exposed; the mistakes and omissions are all my own.

Thanks are due to Panayoti Kelaidis for the loan of some important source material; to Scott Hodges and Justen Wilson of the University of California at Santa Barbara for providing me with papers that I did not quite fully understand; to Sally Walker of Southwestern Native Seeds for her seed collections and for setting me somewhat straight on the aquilegias of Arizona; to Bill Jennings for his slides and his usual perceptive comments; to John White for helping to me understand the complex process of breeding and for illuminating a number of the dark corners in the mysterious world of columbine hybrids; to Dick Bartlett, Ernie Boyd, John Fielding, Charles Mann, Chuck Sheviak, and Randy Tatroe for use of their slides; to Carolyn Crawford for her line drawings; and to my wife for putting up with yet another project, and, of course, for her watercolors.

CHAPTER 1

Cultivation

E VER SINCE the first gardeners turned the earth, columbines have been "set and sowne in gardens for the beautie and variable colour of the floures" (John Parkinson, *Paradisi in Sole Paradisus Terrestris*, 1629). From this one can infer, I hope, that growing columbines is one of life's less difficult tasks. Gardeners—even though they may often turn to the most hermetic instructions for successful gardening, and pass them on to others with relish—probably secretly prefer, as a breed, plants that give the most reward for the least amount of effort.

So, here the mysteries of growing columbines are fully revealed for the first time. Buy a plant, dig a hole in any old soil in full sun or dappled shade, put the plant in the hole, push dirt around the plant, and water it. If the plant is large, it might bloom the same year it is planted; otherwise, it is not unreasonable to expect flowers the second year after planting. There are some notable exceptions, of course, but, judging from the number of columbines that can be seen flourishing in what are obviously casual gardens during a typical spring's drive-by garden visits, most columbines are as easy to grow as petunias and marigolds.

I do not wish to alienate gardeners who are put off by plants that are too easily grown (the favored garden subjects in this country, lawns and hybrid tea roses, are ironically two of the highest-maintenance things anyone could possibly want to grow): some columbines have deserved reputations for being supremely difficult to please; and so to those gardeners who want a challenge, as well as those who like the easy way out—read on.

Columbines can be planted at any time of the year; I am taking for granted that in cold-winter climates the desirability of planting fully dormant plants (which should have a tiny cluster of leaves at the base) during winter is understood. Not too many nurseries are even open for business at this time of year, but supposing they were, and supposing the soil were not a solid block of ice, then planting a clump of roots with the small huddled winter growth attached would be perfectly acceptable. Most plants transplanted into the open garden in mid-winter will have come, I imagine, from the gardener's cold frames.

Once the basal leaves have begun to unfurl, the chances for frost damage increase, unless, of course, the plants have been grown in an open frame and overwintered in the same conditions in which they are to be planted. Depending on the species, these basal leaves will start to emerge from the tiny, almost hidden clusters at ground level at the first sign of warmth in late winter, and they may sit, waiting patiently and half-unfurled, for a month or more until the weather stabilizes (if climates actually exist in which spring offers stable weather), or until they can stand it no longer and finally start to grow, come what may. Studies have shown that these basal leaves are extremely cold-tolerant, so if the plants have already been acclimated to the garden, there should be no need for concern.

I suppose that some would say columbines need fertilizer. Thanks, maybe, to a highly developed laziness that I acquired after many years of gardening, I rarely fertilize any plants (the sole exception is noted below), so I would not know if they need fertilizer. My guess is that if the plants get along in the wild without fertilizer then they probably get along fine without it in the garden, but the psychological effect of doing something (even if it is of no noticeable benefit to the plants) occasionally makes gardeners feel better than if they did nothing at all.

Having said all this, especially the part about "any old soil," I must admit that a more porous soil offers better results, at least initially, than one of heavy clay. Most gardeners do not have ideal garden soil (nor would even years of digging in organic matter achieve this circumstance if the soil starts out like modeling clay), but of course good soil can be spread over the clay. This can be expensive. In arid or semi-arid regions a porous soil will dry out so fast as to require almost daily watering, adding to the expense—and not a little to the gardener's frustrations.

When buying plants in person, you would do well to inspect the root ball. This is probably best done when no one else is looking, although if you make a lot of interested and appreciative noises as you inspect the root ball it may make no difference. In an ideally grown plant the roots should not be too tightly congested, but the ideal is not always attained; if what you see when you pull the pot away from the plant is nothing but a mass of roots, the roots will have to be soaked in water for a few minutes, then ever so gently pulled apart and then planted. This way the roots will not strangle each other as they wind around and around the root ball. In yet another fatal scenario, the roots still dry out instantly, and the plant dies before you know it.

Watering young plants is critical. Newly planted plants should receive water at least every other day, every day if planted during a hot summer. Close attention to the plants when they are young will make for a much healthier plant and less stressful gardening.

Some species seem to betray the genus's reputation for winter hardiness. I have had some trouble overwintering *Aquilegia fragrans* (this is a fancy way of saying it has never made it through a single winter in my garden, with or without protection); I have lost *A. skinneri* even in fairly mild winters, and I have heard that some gardeners have difficulty with the California species *A. eximia*, which I have never grown to maturity (this is an elitist way of saying that I killed it before it even had a chance).

How you protect a plant during the winter is a matter of personal preference. My experience is that anything that has a tendency to get wet in winter (like leaves or straw) will become matted down onto the crown of the plant and cause rot. One method that has worked pretty well here is using a small peat pot, overturned and with the top cut out; the pot is anchored with three long nails and filled with Styrofoam peanuts (a commodity any gardener who orders plants by mail will have in profusion). The peanuts are then held in place with duct tape.

Young plants face a number of horrors as winter approaches. Too much moisture around the crowns, not only from water collecting in mulches, like those just mentioned, but from poor drainage or excessive rain, may cause fatalities. A more likely cause of death may be attributed to the opposite condition: roots that are too dry make it difficult for a plant to sustain long periods of cold weather. Even though the plants are dormant, the roots still need to take up a little moisture, however slight.

The principal cause of dry roots is that plants fail to become established before the onset of winter. The roots of newly planted, successfully established plants will have begun to grow into the surrounding garden soil. This may take a few months, or it may take years. Or it may never happen. By the time the gardener discovers that a plant has failed in its attempts to become established, a swift and terrible death has overtaken the poor thing. The recriminations that follow may be averted at the start: simply remove the soilless mix surrounding the roots of a new plant and plant the plant in the garden soil, whatever that may be. Gently backfill with this same soil, and, in a sense, the roots are already in contact with the existing soil.

I think this method is, as they say, counsel of perfection for gardeners planting in cold-winter climates any time after about 1 October. It has worked for me over and over again, and I never see a plant-pot-shaped ball of soilless mix heaved straight out of the ground, by the action of frost, and heartlessly exposed to the elements. Still, I must say that for every plant I set in the ground this way, there are probably several hundred that are just jammed into the soil any which way, and those plants probably do as well as mine.

Winter hardiness itself is a complex issue that, I think, is scarcely addressed by the U.S. Department of Agriculture Plant Hardiness Zones. Minimum winter temperature is so often the least significant factor in plant survival that it is difficult to assign hardiness ratings to plants. Rainy winters will have different effects on dormant plants, depending upon whether or not a blanket of snow covers the garden for months on end, and sunny, cold, and dry winters offer yet another challenge to plants. From the plant's perspective, spending a winter under a blanket of snow is probably best; we tend to forget that what plants like best might not be what we as humans like best. Too much rain can rot roots, too much sun and wind can desiccate plant crowns; there seems to be no happy medium favorable both to humans and plants, except, of course, in parts of the world where columbines rarely grow. Keeping the crowns slightly moist, but not subjected to awful low temperatures or burning sun, sounds like the ideal to me. And yet . . . the plants grow, regardless of what the weather brings, and equally regardless of the gardener's frantic attempts to kill the plants by overly solicitous measures, whatever they may be.

Columbines suitable for the rock garden are a bit of a different story. Speaking of certain of these plants and "ease of culture" in the same breath will raise more than a few eyebrows. Farrer (1919), who possibly could have stated it more succinctly, said that "some of the most lovely queens" required "a very rich soil that shall always be perfectly porous and sweet [i.e., on the alkaline side] and light, crumbling and never caking, spongy with vegetable matter, freely loosened with an admixture of chips, and sharply drained with the most unfailing and absolute precision." Such are the paces gardeners in rainy climates (with something to drain) are put through, maybe.

"This noble plant," wrote Henri Correvon, a rock gardener and nurseryman, of *Aquilegia alpina*, "is not at all amenable to cultivation" (Correvon and Robert 1911), a complaint echoed through the decades by many of the most expert gardeners. William Robinson (1900) suggested that it was "the alpine character of the home of many of the Columbines which makes the culture of some of the lovely kinds so uncertain," and said that the best soil for them was a "deep, well drained, rich alluvial loam." No doubt every nursery in Robinson's day carried alluvial loam especially for growing columbines.

Of the "lovely queens," *Aquilegia jonesii*, undisputed aristocrat of the genus by any standard, is notoriously difficult to grow well in most climates, and *A. scopulorum* and some others may also prove intractable in some conditions. Most alpine plants can be accommodated if grown in scree; this can be created by mixing equal parts fine gravel, sand, and good garden loam, and mulching the plants with a coarser gravel, such as pea gravel. Other scree formulas should be equally acceptable. A north-facing slope (in the northern hemisphere) will require less watering than one facing south.

Aquilegia jonesii seems to have fairly specific requirements that may be impossible for many gardeners to duplicate: low humidity, high light intensity, alkaline soil, and heat. I grow some of my plants in unamended, dry clay soil, and the plants are rarely watered, even in summers that bring next to no rainfall. If I remember to, I give the plants a blossom-booster-type water-soluble fertilizer in late February. The blossom booster is said to duplicate the minerals the plants get from melting snow in spring. More often than not my plants do without it, and they bloom just as well either way.

The life span of columbines in the garden varies a little with the species. Some, like *Aquilegia chrysantha*, seem to be fairly long-lived; others, like *A. coerulea* and *A. vulgaris*, may last three or four years and then die, leaving dozens of seedlings. The biennial nature of some columbines should not, I hope, detract from our desire to grow them, so long as we understand the plants' intentions to give up the ghost at just the time we are planning to show off our garden to visitors. "Perhaps," wrote Correvon, "the secret is that most die a natural death, the plant being a biennial, so that no care can avoid annual renewal from seed—a thing, fortunately, most easy to do" (Correvon and Robert 1911). The perceived long life span of many columbines may be attributed to their tendency to scatter seeds, and thus seedlings, everywhere around the parent plants, giving the impression that the plants are living forever, which, in a way, they are.

Deadheading (removing the spent flowers) is essential to ensure that columbines, regardless of species, have a reasonable life span in the garden. The flowering stalk should be cut down as soon as the flowers have faded. If you want to save seed, do so on a plant you can spare; plants spend a great deal of energy producing seed, and this energy is best devoted to producing new basal growth for next year, which may not occur if the plants produce a large quantity of seed. Seed can be saved by tying a small cotton bag, available at kitchen-supply stores, around the seed heads. This way the seed will not blow away five minutes before you plan to collect it.

One final observation on the matter of soil: pH. I have already mentioned a preference for alkaline soil twice, once when quoting Farrer, and readers will note that, over and over again in the chapter on the species, most of the species (and by extension their hybrids) grow on calcareous soils in the wild. This does not mean that they have to settle for alkaline soil and really wish they were growing in acidic garden soil; it means that this is the type of soil in which they were born and in which they have speciated over the centuries. If you have an acid soil and want to grow columbines (especially *Aquilegia jonesii*), then adding some horticultural limestone is essential.

18

CHAPTER 2

Pests and Diseases

$\backsim$

THE SECOND THING that people learn after taking up gardening and discovering the first thing (how easy it all really is) is that in setting out a lot of plants in the yard they are often unwittingly creating a gigantic cafeteria for an unimaginable host of insects and bacteria. This is a major and ineluctable fact of gardening life; few things are so absurd as the image of a gardener planting hundreds of plants and then going berserk trying to kill everything that, by natural design, wants to visit them, for good or ill.

Although I do draw the line at blister beetles (which attack clematis and pulsatillas, but not, so far as I have noticed, columbines), I generally leave bugs alone. No doubt I am deluded in some way into thinking that good gardening practices (proper watering, cleaning up dead leaves and other material, not putting shade plants in the sun and vice versa) will keep plants fairly free from diseases and pests; I do very little in the way of pest control, or anything else, for that matter. Since we have dogs, I do not use chemicals of any kind in the garden.

Columbines are not subject to many diseases or pests, at least where I live, although powdery mildew can be a problem at times. Even in a dry climate such as mine this affliction can spoil the appearance of the plants after mid-summer, and other gardeners in the house (usually functioning as resident critics) may continually point out the hideous appearance of mildewed plants, so it is to the gardener's advantage to control mildew. This is not always as easy as it sounds. I use Bordeaux Mixture on occasion, but most times I just look the other way. Mildew unseen is mildew unknown.

A solution of castile soap and water, say a couple of tablespoons of shaved bar soap to a gallon (3.78 l) of water, is said to work well for blackspot on roses; one day I intend to try it on powdery mildew on columbines. The theory behind this is that the fungus (blackspot) needs an acidic leaf cuticle to survive, and the soap solution alkalinizes the cuticle, causing the fungus to die. I know of a least one rosarian who swears by this soap spray. The application is made about twice a week during the summer. Since I have never tried this, it would be a good idea to test-spray a few leaves the day before application, just to check for leaf damage.

Chemical fungicides are available for mildew control, of course; these should be used according to the manufacturer's directions and with consideration for neighbors who might not want to be sprayed. Spraying should be done on a windless day. County extension agents and people in similar positions can assist in choosing the right chemical for the job.

Leaf miners will disfigure leaves now and then with their trails winding through the leaves. The leaf miner is the larva of a fly that lays eggs on the undersides of the leaves. I am unable to find a recommended control, which is possibly just as well. I have had trouble only with the thick-leaved *Aquilegia flabellata* in this regard, and since I am a lazy gardener, I let the leaf miners dig for their green treasure and look the other way.

When it comes to contemplation of the columbine, there is no denying the negative influence the aphid has had on the perceptions of many gardeners. Aphids are probably the worst pest of columbines, finding the hybrids, particularly those with *Aquilegia vulgaris* in their parentage, especially juicy and delicious. A bad aphid infestation can be just about the most disheartening thing imaginable for a gardener whose garden is filled with columbines. I would point out that a lot of popular garden plants are afflicted with an even larger array of destructive pests, roses being the most obvious example, and it is rare to hear of a person not wanting to grow roses despite the frequently ghastly visitations to which they are subject.

Typical symptoms of aphid infestation include stunting of new growth, sticky spots from dripping aphid honeydew on the basal leaves, and hideously deformed flowers—in the event that the flowers do even have enough energy to open. Once again, I take a position of cowardice and prefer not to use a systemic poison. A mixture of liquid castile soap, about 2 tablespoons (30 ml) to a quart (0.946 l) of water, is effective, as are the commercially available pyrethrin sprays. Both kill only on contact and need to be reapplied at every sign of infestation. The castile soap may cause some burning of leaves and should be washed off with water an hour or so after application. Spraying the plants with water will dislodge the aphids, too . . . for a while.

It is best not to look the other way when aphids attack. They do a great deal of damage in a very short time and are a potential vector of viruses, which can quickly spoil the appearance of plants. What is more, aphids procreate at a fantastic rate, and an unchecked infestation can lead to a major trauma in the garden. Aphids do not just like columbines and roses but other plants as well.

Does it go without saying that plants that are well cared for—watered when necessary, deadheaded when necessary, and not horribly shaded by huge leaves—are better prepared to endure the onslaught of pests and diseases than those that are not?

In a cosmic sense, it hardly matters whether or not the gardener has sprayed on a regular schedule or picked aphids off with tweezers. The worst pest of all, the weather, usually makes mincemeat of the flowers just as they are about to open, as it does to almost every garden plant that has the audacity to bloom during the year. I sometimes put wire cages around the best plants, cages which are cunningly constructed to protect the flowers against everything that might happen except what actually does happen.

CHAPTER 3

Propagation

$\backsim$

FOR GARDENERS, propagation of columbines is simple. Unlike many other members of the Ranunculaceae, columbine seed does not appear to have a short life span and need not be sown fresh. Fresh seed, however, will germinate fairly quickly; Nau (1996) says germination can occur within ten to twenty days. Temperatures of 70 to 75F (21 to 24C) are recommended, with the seed exposed to light. Constant inspection of the seeds is mandatory, except in a greenhouse where misting technology is employed. In four or five weeks the seedlings will be ready to be transplanted to larger pots.

Seed can be sown indoors in winter, subjected to nighttime temperatures of 50 to 55F (10 to 13C), and transplanted some time within fifteen to twenty-two weeks, depending on the variety (Nau 1996).

Seed can also be sown by the home gardener in mid-winter outdoors, or subjected to about three weeks of cold treatment in the refrigerator at roughly 40F (5C). Refrigerator treatment can start as late as April. Subjecting seed to cold treatment to promote germination is called vernalization; this is certainly the easiest method for the gardener with little spare time. Occasionally germination of winter-sown seed will be delayed for two years, although in my experience this is not too common.

Munz (1946) recommended mid-summer sowing; this is something I have not tried, although sowing at this time of year is often recommended in horticultural texts. Munz also suggested sowing in early spring for bloom later the same year, which may be the most fantastically optimistic statement I have ever read (he does go on to say that such plants "are not apt to do so" . . . indeed). In dry-summer regions, with seed sown at any time other than winter, irrigation would obviously be necessary; in my experience, keeping young seedlings alive during extended periods of drought (which essentially defines my gardening conditions) is a considerable chore.

Robinson (1900), who wrote, of course, with the benefit of an equable climate (not to mention resources that included old garden frames and cloudy days) also recommended spring sowing: "The seeds should be sown early in spring, and the young plants pricked out into pans or an old garden frame as soon as they are fit to handle, removing them early in August to the borders; select a cloudy day for the work, and give them a little shading for a few days."

A good soilless mix for a germination medium is equal parts sand, perlite, and decomposed organic material, preferably with minimal peat content. Peat, especially when contained in constantly watered pots, tends to break down over time, and if the tap water used is even slightly on the alkaline side, the combination of acidic peat moss (granulated sphagnum peat) and alkaline water can lead to a really disgusting mess in less than two years. If we recall our basic chemistry (ignoring, perhaps, how poorly we performed in class), we know that an acid plus a base equals a salt plus water; the presence of these salts in growing media is something definitely undesirable. The soilless mix can be made at home, or a commercial potting compost with leaf mold or something similar can be purchased, which may produce better results. I usually just throw in whatever I have on hand and mix it together more or less thoroughly. The results are pretty much the same whether you use a scientifically blended mix or just improvise. Here I have one of the few advantages that a dry climate offers: fungal diseases and pathogens in potting mixes are rare, even with salvaged potting soil.

The seeds are sown on top of the soilless mix and lightly pressed into the mix. The pots are then left to stand in a pan full of water, so that the mix absorbs the water from the bottom; this may take an hour or so. The mix can be judged to have been thoroughly moistened simply by lifting the pot and weighing it by hand. It is a popular misconception that seeds will explode, or die, if frozen the night they are sown. I routinely sow columbine seeds during subfreezing weather with no ill effects (except on me).

Once the seeds have fully imbibed, it is imperative that they not dry out again. The seeds may not actually die, but they may be forced into an even deeper dormancy, one that would require the kiss of a frog prince to overcome. A thin topdressing of fine gravel is perfect for ensuring protection of the seeds; it keeps the pots moist during dry spells and prevents the young seedlings from being washed out by rain. There should be as little space as possible between the top of the gravel and the top of the pot; this prevents the disasters that can occur after prolonged winter thaws. When the soilless mix has thawed in the top portion, and the lower portion of the pot is still frozen, drainage is impaired and water pools at the top of the pot. The seeds rot. The ideal is to keep the pots fully frozen, or, if that is not possible, at least to keep the layer of gravel so high that no water pools on top. When not frozen, the seed pots will need plenty of moisture from spring to autumn; this is probably best done with a watering can equipped with a fine rose that does not, we can always hope, fall off at just the wrong moment.

Outdoor germination of seeds (keeping pots outside all winter in cold-winter climates) is an idea that meets with considerable resistance, especially in gardeners who have never tried it. Nature does this, so there is no real reason for people to view this method with such suspicion. If the seedlings come up too early and get frosted, what then? Well, they get frosted, recover, and go about their business. Hardy plants have hardy seedlings.

Another method, safer in some ways and less so in others, is to sow the seeds in pots and then place the pots in the refrigerator, possibly after a considerable amount of bargaining or pleading with other members of the household. Plastic sandwich bags are fitted over the pots to keep them moist. The biggest problem with this method is fungus, which can ruin the whole project in no time at all. Powdered charcoal is semi-effective against fungus; a little dusting over the top of the gravel may be all that is necessary. The best prevention, though, is daily inspection of the pots. (And since we are suddenly in the refrigerator, there may be other things to find as well . . .) The pots are then set outdoors, say some time in mid-May, or even earlier in more agreeable climates than mine, and the seeds will often germinate quite quickly afterward.

Columbines can also be germinated indoors under lights, after having received the necessary cold treatment, although the plants may tend to become spindly unless the growing lights are quite close to the tops of the pots (less than 6 inches, 15 cm). This is a staggering amount of work and best left, in my view, to those who are otherwise idle. Young plants are also less easily transplanted directly into garden conditions than those grown outdoors; plants grown outdoors need no extensive hardening-off period and can be set directly into the garden even in freezing weather.

Hardening-off is a tedious process. Young plants whose only home has been the comfort of a warm bed under lights will object in the strongest way possible to being left outside for one frosty night. The acclimatization must be gradual. For the first two weeks or so, the plants should be left in a relatively shady area and taken in during the night. As the nights get warmer, the plants can be left out all night; there is still the possibility of damage if frost should come in early morning. Eventually the plants will have become accustomed to the rigors of outdoor life, and they can be planted into the garden.

In difficult gardening climates, seedlings grown outdoors are much more easily transplanted than either seedlings grown indoors or plants purchased from a greenhouse. This point cannot be stressed enough. Farrer (1907), writing in *My Rock-Garden*, said much the same thing: "Seedlings [are] so much more vigorous than bought plants, as from their birth they are busy adapting themselves to the place they grow in, instead of, like a poor bought plant, making vain efforts to take up the broken strand of life, and forget the place they came from."

Well, not quite, of course. Let no one think that I would ever consider telling gardeners not to buy nursery-grown plants, since my own yearly purchases total to an embarrassingly large percentage of our annual income. Just the opposite: continue to buy plants but also grow plants from seed, in order to reach the ultimate goal of gardening—more, more, and still more plants. Besides, some growers have now reverted to the old-fashioned practice of setting their plants outside once the weather warms, so the plants have a chance to harden off.

Some impatient gardeners like to use chemicals to promote faster germination. Both hydrogen peroxide and gibberellic acid (GA_3) are occasionally recommended for this purpose. Gibberellic acid ($C_{19}H_{22}O_6$)

is a naturally occurring plant hormone that was originally isolated in a fungus of rice and described as *Gibberella fujirokoi*. Various commercial preparations are available, and GA$_3$ has become quite popular both with amateurs and professionals for its ability to overcome seed dormancy by breaking down germination inhibitors. The seeds are treated with GA$_3$ and then germinated in the folds of moist paper towels; after germination the seeds, with their emerging radicles, are carefully transplanted to a growing medium. I have used both GA$_3$ and hydrogen peroxide but have never been quite sure what to do with the resulting tender plants, since I do not have a greenhouse.

One concern—keeping the species, varieties, and cultivars pure in the garden—is not so simply addressed. While some species are moderately self-fertile, the genus is notorious for the interfertility of its individual species, and species readily hybridize with almost any member of their genus, species or cultivar, within sight. Seed resulting from these assignations may or may not come true; if you want something different, then this should not be a problem. In order to maintain purity, it is necessary to construct some sort of chastity belt around the plant. A small cage fashioned out of finely meshed wire, to keep out pollinators, works well. The cage should be put over the plants before they start to flower, naturally.

Once this is done, the flowers can be "selfed" by brushing pollen from the anthers onto the stigma of a flower that opened a few days earlier (the flowers are protandrous, so the anthers shed their pollen a few days before the stigma becomes receptive); a fine watercolor brush is perfectly suited for this operation. Once the seed capsules have formed, the cages can be removed. This is a huge amount of work, by the way, and, as far as I am concerned, having never tried it with columbines, theory and not practice.

Increasing plants by division is possible; plants can be gently prized apart in late winter, before new growth starts, and replanted. The success rate will not be great, for as George Schenk (1984) has observed, "columbine transplants uneasily"; this is because the roots tend to delve deeply, and the feeder roots may be beyond the reach of a spade. "Certain it is that columbines are prodigious rooters, the stock [i.e., of the root], it may be, boring two feet before emitting roots" (Correvon and Robert 1911). Transplanting any plant without feeder roots is a sure path to failure. The holes required both for digging up existing plants and for transplanting must be large enough, to use Schenk's memorable phrase, "to bury a wheelbarrow with dignity." Young plants, of course, require no extreme measures except care in handling the tender roots.

In the commercial greenhouse, where columbines are grown not for the gardening trade but as potted plants or for the cut flower trade, the situation is vastly different. For one thing, there is a greater sense of urgency in bridging the time gap between seed sowing and flower production. Where a weekend gardener like myself can afford to wait two years for seedlings to appear, in commercial production this would be a disaster, and so various techniques are employed to hasten flowering. Some of the F_1 hybrids, notably those of the Songbird series, offer the commercial grower the tremendous advantage of not requiring vernalization treatments, which means flowering plants are produced within an acceptable time frame.

Experiments have shown that applications of GA_3, especially, shorten the period between initial development of the flower stalk and flower production; plants were brought to initialization of flower buds about four and a half months after the seed was sown (Zhang 1987). Other methods of hastening flowering—a period of cold treatment or extension of photoperiod by subjecting the plants to high light intensity for eighteen hours a day—were also effective, but not as effective as periodic applications of GA_3.

Morphology and Distribution

$\backsim$

*A*quilegia is a member of the buttercup family (Ranunculaceae), an overly large, unnecessarily complicated, and broadly defined family, the members of which can have leaves that are simple or compound; flowers that are usually bisexual, with no petals or lots of them, about ten stamens or lots of them, and one pistil or lots of them; and fruit that can be an achene, a berry, or a follicle, with one seed or lots of them. Some other well-known, commonly cultivated genera in this family are *Aconitum* (monkshood), *Actaea, Anemone, Caltha, Clematis, Consolida* (larkspur), *Delphinium, Eranthis, Helleborus, Nigella, Pulsatilla, Ranunculus, Thalictrum,* and *Trollius.*

The genus *Aquilegia* is sometimes put in a separate family, Helleboraceae, proposed by Loiseleur in 1819, where the fruit is (almost) always a follicle, but most botanists have continued to include *Aquilegia* in the buttercup family.

The most familiar flower shape of all, that of *Aquilegia coerulea*, is not exactly the standard throughout the genus. Some columbine flowers are small, some are nodding, some have hooked spurs, some have long straight spurs, some have no spurs at all. I would not go as far as Munz (1946) did in suggesting that that there are "few groups of plants richer in the variety of their offering," since there are few genera with more recognizable flower structures, and whose nomenclature, when based solely at looking at individual specimens, is as uncertain. The difference of opinion here, I should add, is due to my own limitations rather than to those

Leaf structures, biternate (left) and triternate.
Drawing by Carolyn Crawford.

of Munz, who possessed a finer eye for detail than I could ever hope to have.

Typically, the plant has a tuft of usually long-petioled basal leaves comprised of multiple leaflets; the leaves may be ternately (in groups of three) compound, biternately (doubly ternate) compound, or triternately (triply ternate) compound. Most *Aquilegia* species have biternate leaves, in which the three divisions of a ternate leaf are themselves divided into three parts. Close examination of the leaflets may help to identify those species that are distinguished by the presence or absence of microscopic hairs; by the presence of glands, which cause the leaflets to feel sticky (viscid or glutinous) to the touch; or by a kind of glaucous "bloom," caused by the presence of a waxy leaf cuticle.

The stems usually have cauline leaves that become increasingly simple toward the inflorescence. Close examination of the stems will reveal the same set of characteristics that distinguish the leaflets (hairs, glands, bloom—or not). Very occasionally there are species whose adaptations to exceptional climates have caused the leaflets to be crowded among themselves, so that the plant forms a cushion of basal leaves with practically no visible stems. The species with crowded leaflets are unmistakable: *Aquilegia jonesii* (the most extravagant example), *A. laramiensis*, *A. saximontana*, and *A. scopulorum*, all North American; and the Siberian *A. borodinii*.

The buds, nodding at first even on species with erect flowers, are on branches having leafy bracts. The flower consists of five petaloid sepals, five petals alternating with the sepals, and a group of stamens, which are conspicuously exserted in many species, especially in North America. The central stamens usually are reduced to flattened staminodes.

The sepals, sometimes called perianth segments, are held at various angles to the floral axis (the angle created by the line from the pedicel through the center of the flower: a flower with sepals held straight out has the sepals perpendicular to the floral axis). Sepals are characterized as spreading if they are held at any angle to the floral axis between about 45 and 90 degrees. If not, they are divergent—unless they stick out just slightly, when they are judged, rather bizarrely, to be erect. Species with spreading sepals must be identified when the flower is fully opened; otherwise, of course, the sepals will appear divergent, on their way to opening fully.

The petals, which are sometimes called honey-leaves, consist of two parts. Each petal has an elongated spur containing nectar (so much so, in some species, that a pressed specimen stains the page with nectar); the spurs may be straight, curved or hooked, or coiled. They may even be entirely lacking, or saccate, in which case they appear as rounded bumps (and in which case we would look to another set of characteristics for positive identification).

The absence of spurs is attributed to a recessive gene. Some spurred species often produce populations in the wild entirely lacking spurs; the absence of spurs in normally spurred species must make pollination difficult for these plants, which have occasionally been given taxonomic status. As we shall see in the chapter on hybrids, when spurless plants are crossed with spurred plants, the offspring produce spurs in the normal manner.

The nectar-filled spurs, from which the genus probably gets its name, are the business end of the flower from the point of view of the pollinators. The Eurasian species are pollinated mostly by flies, bees, and bumblebees; those in North America are pollinated by bees, bumblebees, hawkmoths (*Aquilegia coerulea, A. chrysantha,* and *A. pubescens*), and, in the red-flowered species, hummingbirds.

The spurs elongate into blades, or laminae, which may be held at various angles to the floral axis but are generally relatively straight, and may be narrow or wide, or, again, completely lacking. Some botanists have suggested that plants in dry climates have no need to protect their pollen and can therefore face upward, which would be one explanation for the presence of blades surrounding the stamens, but in some species in which the stamens are completely unprotected (*Aquilegia eximia,* for example), the flowers face downward.

The flowers have multiple stamens. Many of these are actually a bundle of flattened golden staminodes, often quite visible, especially in many North American species; these sometimes extend beyond the end of the blades, in which case they are described as exserted. Staminodes that do not quite reach the end of the blades are said to be included. The length of the staminodes relative to the end of the blades may be an important diagnostic feature.

The fruit is a follicle, splitting open on one side, with a curling "beak" at the tip. The follicles are generally held upright and are often used in differentiation between species, along with other characteristics.

The seeds, so familiar to many gardeners, are numerous and glistening black.

As will be mentioned more than once, the species in the genus *Aquilegia* generally have a high rate of interfertility, but distinct characteristics among the species act as barriers to pollination in populations of species whose ranges overlap. Columbines are to an extent self-fertile, but the examples of plants produced by self-fertilization, compared to those in which the offspring was the result of cross-pollination with another plant in the same species, clearly indicate a preference for the latter method of reproduction (Proctor et al. 1996).

Columbines, as species, are allopatric, that is to say, species are rarely found growing together. Their territory is usually marked by preference for a particular habitat and by a difference in the pollinators they attract. In Eurasia very short, spurred plants seem to be the rule at the highest elevations (*Aquilegia moorcroftiana, A. nivalis*), possibly in response to the size of the flies or bees that visit them. In regions where two species might be present but are separated by a difference in habitat (say, by elevation), one species might have straight spurs and the other, hooked spurs; or the flower color is such that the plants attract different pollinators.

Introgression between two species with different pollinators may be caused by a third animal that displays no favoritism toward either species. In his study of introgression between *Aquilegia formosa* and *A. pubescens*, Grant (1952) noted that bumblebees were seen loaded with pollen on a plant of the hummingbird-pollinated *A. formosa*. These apparently are the agents of the first crossing between the two species; subsequent introgression is then carried out by hummingbirds on the formosa-type plants and hawkmoths on the pubescens-type plants.

The predominant flower color in the genus is blue, or some shade of blue to purple to almost black, colors favored by bees and flies. Only a few species in Europe and Asia lack blue or purple coloration; only one (*Aquilegia aurea*) is yellow. In North America the principal colors are yellow and red; only the high-elevation species have a blue or blue-purple color, with the exception of *A. pubescens*.

The pale-colored species, particularly in North America, are especially favored by hawkmoths; it has been conjectured that these flowers—being visible to humans at twilight, when the darker-flowered species are not—might also be more visible to the hawkmoths, which are their principal pollinators (Grant 1952).

Columbines are distributed throughout the northern hemisphere in temperate regions, mostly growing on calcareous limestone soils. Speciation seems to be concentrated in southern Europe, especially, if we are to take all the recent descriptions seriously, in the countries constituting the former Yugoslavia; new species are being described there almost yearly, it seems. Some botanists have told me that there may be several undescribed species in Arizona and possibly northern Mexico as well; if this is so, then the hottest region in North America will lay claim to having the greatest number of columbine species.

In a rough estimate, the countries comprising the former Yugoslavia have at least ten species, Italy has eight, France six, Austria four, Greece and Switzerland three, Spain and Bulgaria two. Utah has at least ten species; Arizona, Colorado, and Wyoming have six; Texas five; California, Nevada, and New Mexico have four. The mountainous region of the Tien Shan, curving in a northeasterly direction around western China through the Altai Mountains, is also especially rich in species.

The preference in all sunny climates seems to be for streamsides, woodland glades, or shady overhangs (the "hanging gardens" of western North America), not roasting on barren sand or rock. Columbines are not xerophytes, although the alpine species naturally grow in drier locations than species favoring lower elevations.

Columbines in North America, especially, are "invader" plants that came across the Bering Strait land bridge from Asia. If we accept the hypothesis that *Aquilegia vulgaris* is the ancestral species, then they came a long way indeed; or, as is also possible (the strongly similar species *A. olympica, A. karelinii, A. sibirica,* and *A. oxysepala* suggesting a wider presence of *A. vulgaris* at a much earlier period in the evolution of the columbine), the march of the species was not so far as all that. The closest relative to *A. vulgaris*—in appearance—in North America is *A. brevistyla,* whose distribution pattern is south and east from Alaska into British Columbia, Manitoba, and ultimately the Black Hills of South Dakota. Taylor (1967) showed that *A. brevistyla* crossed more readily with the North American species than with those with which it had apparent close relationships (*A. sibirica,* for example), but perhaps this is an evolutionary trait brought about by a change in pollinator species, or perhaps *A. brevistyla* is the result of an ancient intermingling with another North American species.

The species pollinated by hummingbirds in North America show an obvious pattern. There is one red-flowered species, *Aquilegia canadensis,* in eastern North America, and one species of hummingbird, the ruby-throated hummingbird (*Archilochus colubris*); *A. canadensis* is one of the most important hummingbird plants in eastern North America (Proctor et al. 1996). West and south of the Rocky Mountains, the species of hummingbirds begin to increase, as do the number of red-flowered columbine species.

Curiously, the more advanced (or less primitive) species *Aquilegia formosa,* pollinated by hummingbirds, shows the same pattern, with the bulk of its populations in California. It may be an illusion to suggest that here the pattern is reversed, with the species moving into Alaska rather than out of it. The supposed existence of *A. formosa* in Kamchatka makes this idea even more attractive, but there are no hummingbirds in Kamchatka, or, at least, there had better not be. In any case, it is true that with *A. brevistyla*, a bee-pollinated species with hooked spurs, the bulk of the populations show a larger distribution in a direction that makes them appear to be coming into North America, while with *A. formosa*, a hummingbird-pollinated species with straight spurs, the distribution makes them look as though they are slowly moving out of North America.

The same pattern—a primitive species appearing to fan out in a direction toward more advanced species—is not readily apparent where the Eurasian species of *Aquilegia* are concerned. This is probably because the most evolved agent of selection, the hummingbird, is a creature confined to the New World. Many European species show a distinct, even excessive, similarity to *Aquilegia vulgaris*, with the exception of a happy few that choose to align themselves with *A. alpina* instead. In Asia, probably the most extreme example of speciation, especially in its distinctly odd coloration, is *A. viridiflora*, but even it in no way exhibits the extremes of adaptation displayed by the bladeless California species *A. eximia* or by *A. jonesii*, the cushion plant.

CHAPTER 5

Doves and Eagles

VER SINCE Linnaeus named the genus in 1753 (in *Species Plantarum*), the derivation of the word *aquilegia* has been the subject of speculation. The most commonly suggested explanation is that it is from the Latin *aquila* ("eagle"), a supposed reference to the resemblance of the blades to an eagle's wing, or to the hooked spurs resembling an eagle's claw. The word *aquilegia*, in fact, was in use, in one form or another, as a common name for these plants long before Linnaeus chose it for the generic name. The old English herbals used the extremely eagle-like name of *aquilina* with some frequency; in his 1629 classic, Parkinson wrote, "All later Writers doe generally call it eyther *Aquileia*, *Aquilina*, or *Aquilegia*."

In Old High German, at least seven hundred years before *Species Plantarum*, the word was *agaleia* (Damboldt 1965). Permutations like *acoleia* and *agleia* were known in Germany in the twelfth century. The theory that *aquilegia* is a translation of the German name is an interesting one, since the Old High German word is reasonably close to the Middle English *egle*. But in modern German, the word for columbine is *akelei*, which has no relationship to the modern German word for eagle, *adler*; and, of course, words that sound alike do not necessarily share the same root.

Although this will be an unpopular statement, the often-repeated association of the word *aquilegia* with *aquila* is not only implausible, it is demonstrably incorrect. No explanation has ever been given for the mysterious suffix -*egia*, which would have to be appended arbitrarily to the name, and there is no word in Latin with this ending meaning eagle.

There is a word, or a group of words, with this ending in Latin, however, and surely Linnaeus saw that the derivation of the word he chose for the genus was from *aquilex* (plural *aquileges*), "dowser," or "water finder," referring to the quantity of nectar in the spurs (especially evident in the pressed specimens of some species). *Aquilex* is composed of two words, *aqua* ("water") and *legere* ("to lead," "to draw"). Bulavkina, author of the treatment of *Aquilegia* in *Flora of the U.S.S.R.* (1937), notes that the Russian name *vodosbor* ("aquilegia") is a literal translation of *aqua* and *legere*. Another possibility is *aquilegus* ("water collector").

I think it is correct to say that *aquilegia* comes from *aquilex*, but the older popular names may have come from words meaning eagle. In other words, despite the similarity of the words *agaleia* and *aquilegia*, they probably had nothing to do with each other except that they referred to the same plant. It is difficult, for me at least, to connect anything having to do with eagles with the delicate, and definitely un-eagle-like, columbine.

Dioscorides called it *Isopyrum*, a generic name still in use, and one to which some columbines, formerly of the genus *Aquilegia*, are occasionally whisked away, never to be seen again. Parkinson notes that Theophrastus called it *Diosanthos* ("flower of the gods") or *Pothos*.

The English common name has a number of putative derivations, the most common of these being that the sepals resemble a dove's wing, another being that the five sepals together resemble five doves or pigeons, "with small leaves [i.e., sepals] standing upright, of the shape of little birds" (John Gerard, *Herball*, 1597). Columbine (spelled colombine by Parkinson) is probably the best-known common name; crowsfoot is another. The name granny's bonnet is occasionally applied to forms of *Aquilegia vulgaris*.

The spurs also, of course, look like horns, and the columbine was a symbol of cuckoldry for hundreds of years. Is it coincidence that the columbine was the subject of unseemly reference in English literature, even as it was recognized to be a plant with astonishing sexual proclivities? Are the perceptions of columbines as aphrodisiacs by indigenous peoples of North America likewise attributable to the general salacious image of the columbine?

Hegi's *Illustrierte Flora von Mittel-Europa* (1965) gives about thirty different German names for the plant, among the more fanciful being devil's-bells (*Teufelglocken*), sugar-bells (*Zuckerglocken*), and fool's-cap (*Narrenkappen*). The French sometimes call it Our Lady's glove (*gants-de-Notre-Dame*), the Italians love-born (*amor-nascoto*). This is getting pretty far away from pigeons and doves, to say nothing of eagles.

CHAPTER 6

Taxonomic Tangles

⌀⟋

T HE 1946 monograph by Munz is the standard taxonomic reference for the genus *Aquilegia.* Unfortunately, the author was all too eager to split species into as many varieties as possible; his work covers sixty-seven species and, seemingly, about 300,000 varieties. Modern taxonomists are less willing to recognize the absurd twenty-odd varieties of *Aquilegia vulgaris* that Munz considered acceptable in the mid-twentieth century. Yet even Munz's work was an advance over previous treatments in terms of the lengths, literally, to which taxonomists would go to describe a plant: what we now call *A. formosa* var. *truncata* (or plain *A. formosa,* as it is described in the *Jepson Manual*) was once called (believe it or not) *A. canadensis* subsp. *americana* var. *incarnata* forma *truncata.*

It seems counterproductive to suggest that every slight variation may represent a species or even a variety. We no longer have an E. L. Greene, who believed in the immutability of species and named every specimen he encountered as if it were a distinct taxonomic entity. It is worthwhile to err on the side of caution when assessing the characteristics that define a species. Too rigid a definition may result in a proliferation of varietal names, which only leads to confusion. The components that define a species should always be able to be subjected to reconsideration based on new evidence. For instance, if a species is defined as having entirely glabrous foliage, and specimens are collected that resemble the species in every respect except, say, that they have slightly pubescent foliage, then, rather than describe the specimens as a new variety, the definition of the species itself could be modified to say that the plant has entirely glabrous foliage with occasionally pubescent foliage. In the nineteenth century, especially, the tendency was to recognize the slight difference as a new species or variety, partly because the amount of collected material on which the original description was based was small; but with the large amount of collected material now available, a broader definition of a species is not only justifiable but desirable.

When collected material shows a difference marked by geography, then defense of the redefinition of the species based on the new material is more difficult. The pubescent foliage of my hypothetical specimens may well represent an evolutionary adaptation to cold temperatures or drought, and in this case, a new varietal status may be warranted. Of course, further collections of plants growing within colonies of plants with glabrous foliage may cause the new variety to be rejected.

Modern taxonomy has the benefit of a much more expansive vision of evolutionary adaptation than was available to nineteenth-century botanists (not to mention to botanists working in the eighteenth century), which is one reason why so many species and variety names have disappeared, as the taxa are subjected to constant reevaluation. Modern botanists also, of course, have the advantage of almost instantaneous communication, so that a description of a new species from central Asia is news in Berlin, New York, and Tokyo simultaneously. Still, it is an impressive measure of the acumen of many botanists of the 1800s that the names they gave to so many columbines have stood intact for a century and a half or so.

Current treatments of the genus in various floras are inconsistent beyond belief. Some botanists prefer to recognize every variety, while others subsume all varieties under one species. After studying the floras of regions where columbines grow, and after reading Munz's monograph, I could easily (well, almost easily) be persuaded that the supposed differences in many of the species are not so great that they warrant taxonomic differentiation. This is partly due to the fluidity of the concept of a species; probably no two botanists would agree precisely on the exact definition of a species, since, after all, a species is an abstract concept, and, like other abstractions, is variously defined, depending on who is using the word.

We may well ask ourselves what exactly it is that we mean when we use the word *species*. Definitions abound, and probably no more than two or three people will agree on a definition that fits the views of every field of endeavor in which species are the subject of research. At present I prefer Cronquist's definition: "the smallest groups that are consistently and persistently distinct, and distinguishable by ordinary means" (Gleason and Cronquist 1991). Of course, *consistently*, *persistently*, *distinct*, and *distinguishable* are all heavily loaded words. "Ordinary means" in this case includes inspection with a hand lens.

Readers who are able to plow through the chapter detailing the individual species without having their eyes permanently glaze over will notice a potential for nomenclatural change contained in almost every species. A naming convention, the International Code of Botanical Nomenclature, is now followed almost universally, and, in general, when a name is changed (even a name well worn in horticulture), it is usually for sound reasons. This makes less difference to me than to some people. I do not hesitate to use the new name *Aquilegia turczaninovii* for a thoroughly obscure species, or even the accepted spelling *A. coerulea* for a species spelled *caerulea* everywhere in horticulture, but switching from *A. flabellata* to *A. japonica* is too much even for me.

The constant juggling of names from here to there can be troubling to gardeners who are collectors. Collectors who want every taxon usually acquire them by name. Even though gardeners are constantly warned against the tendency to acquire everything, they seldom pay attention. I speak from experience: collectors wanting every single variety and form found within the genus embark on a voyage of no return.

Not only is the nomenclature in the genus inconsistent (and riddled with synonyms that switch back and forth even within the various treatments like players in a game of musical chairs), and not only do some authorities disagree on the attributes of the taxa in the genus, the genus has also been subjected to the same treatment in horticulture. Neither Farrer nor Clay, to mention just two of the most notable examples, seemed overly concerned with nomenclatural accuracy, and many of their comments are nothing more than conjecture. Certainly no law prohibits guessing when all else has failed (readers who know more about this genus than I do will notice that I indulge in this from time to time), but it should be the exception rather than standard practice.

One objection to name-changing is that many of the plants are already familiar to gardeners under old names, and changing them only creates more confusion. The first piece of information we encounter is usually the one that clings strongest in our imaginations; even if the name is wrong, we tend to resent the idea that the plant whose name we learned first is traveling under false pretenses. With the names in *Aquilegia* in such disarray, it is little wonder that nursery plants have an even chance of being wrongly identified.

The unfortunate habit of giving Latin names to cultivars and selections, a practice that was especially popular in the nineteenth and early twentieth centuries, is now prohibited by the International Code for Nomenclature of Cultivated Plants. Such pseudo-Latin names as, for example, *Aquilegia flabellata nana alba*, or any name that included the words *flore pleno* ("full-flowered," meaning doubled—at least—sepals), are no longer permitted for new cultivars. The old ones are now written as *A. flabellata* 'Nana Alba' (the look of *A. flabellata* cv. Nana Alba was for a time allowed but that too is no longer to be used, per the ICNCP), and so all the old cultivar names appear here in single quotes. There is little else to do but retain them as cultivar names, all the while hoping, no doubt through the far-reaching influence of this book, that their use in Latin binomials and trinomials will rapidly become a thing of the past.

CHAPTER 7

Some Columbine Cousins

⌒

A MONG the columbine cousins we find a welter of names, synonyms, and doubtful relationships—plants that move back and forth between genera like unruly siblings shuffled from family to family by relatives. Gardeners may occasionally come across plants with aquilegia in their names; some of these plants have had to reintroduce themselves so many times, it is a wonder they have the courage to continue growing at all.

The measurements are those taken by various botanists describing the species; rarely are they measurements taken by me. The measurements are consistent throughout the literature—there is only one way to describe spurs that are 11 mm long. I have used the metric system throughout, which may cause concern for some readers, but converting millimeters to inches would clutter up the text in the most horrific way imaginable. One millimeter equals 0.03937 inches, so you can see to what unutterable agony this would lead (not to mention the fact that I would be spending the next thirty years converting millimeters to fractions of an inch). A U.S. dime stood on edge is one millimeter wide. One centimeter is just slightly larger than three-quarters of an inch; 15 centimeters is 6 inches, 30 centimeters is a foot, and so on.

The genus *Semiaquilegia* was proposed in 1902 by the Japanese botanist Makino in order to create a genus, at that time considered unique to Japan and adjacent areas of the Far East, similar to *Aquilegia* but with distinct characteristics: no spurs, fewer than fifteen stamens, and inner stamens that appear as flattened staminodes. Munz rejected Makino's genus in his monograph, hurling *Semiaquilegia adoxoides*, without much comment, into the genus *Isopyrum*, where, I need hardly add, it was when it was first described by de Candolle in 1818.

Semiaquilegia adoxoides was subsumed into *Aquilegia* by Ohwi (1965), but current theory (Hodges and Arnold 1995; Hodges 1997a, 1997b; Dezhi and Robinson 2001) considers *Semiaquilegia* a separate, valid genus, related but not necessarily ancestral to *Aquilegia*. This species, which blooms March to May in the mountains of Japan, Korea, and neighboring areas of China, grows to 40 cm or so, with ternate, slightly glaucous basal leaves and nodding pale pink flowers about 9 mm long. The spurs are saccate, or completely absent. Clay (1937) perhaps unfairly dismissed it as "weedy."

The confusion, however, began a few years earlier, in a paper by Drummond and Hutchinson (1920), the intention of which was to reconsider the chaotic genus *Isopyrum*. One result of this study was the creation of a new genus, *Paraquilegia*, but another result, rather less fortunate, was the expansion of Makino's genus *Semiaquilegia* into a group of four species, *Semiaquilegia adoxoides* and three new half-columbines, *S. eastwoodiae*, *S. henryi*, and *S. simulatrix*. Drummond and Hutchinson considered the absence of a "petal-spur [to be] an important landmark from the phyletic standpoint, in that it indicates the origins of *Aquilegia*." As we shall see, the three new species of *Semiaquilegia* made for strange bedfellows indeed.

The first of these three new half-columbines is a presumably extinct spurless form of *Aquilegia micrantha* found in southwestern Colorado. The taxonomic history of Alice Eastwood's columbine is a peculiar one, and perhaps worth telling. In 1891, Eastwood saw a spurless columbine in Johnston Canyon in Mesa Verde National Park in southwestern Colorado "in but one nichelike cavern, where the sun never comes [this must have been hyperbole considering the obvious presence of chlorophyll in columbines] and where the supply of water is so slight during the hot, dry summer that it is forced to cling close to the damp rocks" (Payson 1918). She described the plant she found as *A. ecalcarata*, unaware that Maximowicz had used this name nine years before.

Two years later, Marcus Jones proposed a new section, Pseudaquilegia, to accommodate Eastwood's columbine, but no one seemed particularly anxious to accept this new section. A few years after this, Eastwood discovered spurred forms of her columbine and called them *Aquilegia micrantha*. Apparently learning that her earlier specific epithet had already been used (the rules of nomenclature require that the first use of a name, with some exceptions, be given precedence), she renamed her spurless plant *A. micrantha mancosana* (*A. micrantha* var. *mancosana* in some current treatments). Rydberg decided to call it *A. eastwoodiae* in his 1906 *Flora of Colorado*, which accounts for its transformation into *Semiaquilegia eastwoodiae* some years later. Eastwood's spurless columbine was last seen in the wild by humans in the autumn of 1892.

The second half-columbine in this group, *Semiaquilegia henryi*, with upward-facing flowers, is now a member of either the genus *Isopyrum* (where it was when first described in 1888; it was also in *Aquilegia* for a few years) or the genus *Urophysa*, depending on which flora is consulted. The new *Flora of China* calls it *Urophysa henryi*.

The last of the group, *Semiaquilegia simulatrix*, is now considered an aquilegia (*Aquilegia ecalcarata*, by which name it was first described) by botanists, but rarely, if ever, so called by horticulturists, who still insist on calling it either the rather euphonious *S. simulatrix* or *S. ecalcarata*. It is, as Drummond and Hutchinson (1920) conceded, "otherwise in general appearance so absolutely a Columbine" that the persistence of horticulture in calling it something other than what it obviously is must be attributed to stubbornness more than anything else. Both Munz and Taylor (1967) reported that this species provides fertile offspring when crossed with another *Aquilegia* species.

The *Flora of the U.S.S.R.* also recognized *Semiaquilegia mandshurica*, which is now *Isopyrum mandshuricum* in the new treatments in *Flora of China*. A species sometimes called *S. rockii* (not to be confused with *Aquilegia rockii*) is also now there as *Urophysa rockii*.

So, to condense these agonizingly italics-ridden few paragraphs into a single sentence, the only species that legitimately belongs in *Semiaquilegia* is *S. adoxoides*. More italics will follow shortly.

The other genus, *Paraquilegia*, segregated out of the genus *Isopyrum* by Drummond and Hutchinson in 1920, is a small group of species of central Asian cushion plants found at high elevations from northern Iran, in the Elburz Mountains, through Afghanistan and eastward into the

Himalayas and northward into the Tien Shan and Mongolia. The generic name means "next to" or "beside" *Aquilegia*, and these plants, while they may bear leaves that conspicuously resemble those of columbines, have upward-facing spurless flowers with no staminodes, and the appearance of the flowers is more akin to anemones than to columbines. Rechinger (1992) considered *Paraquilegia* to be homologous in development to that of *Dionysia* in the Primulaceae.

Possibly the most notable thing about paraquilegias is the way they are spoken of by serious rock gardeners, in hushed and awed voices; these are strictly plants for the most experienced growers who are able to give them the conditions they require (a north-facing crevice garden, for instance). Of the columbines themselves, only *Aquilegia jonesii* is their equal in aristocratic demeanor and tendency to sulk in the garden. Farrer (1919) described, perhaps immodestly and definitely prolixly, what he called *Isopyrum farreri* (now considered a horticultural form of *Paraquilegia anemonoides*; both Farrer and Clay discuss these gems under the genus *Isopyrum*) thus: "In the fast crevices it forms cushions of dainty leafage of greyish-blue, more than a foot [30 cm] across, covered in due time with a profusion of gold-fluffed flowers like miniature Meconopsids of lavender, or purple tinge, balancing on single fine stems of 2 or 3 inches [50 to 75 mm], in such profusion as to hide the mass from which they spring." The comment by Clay (1937), that paraquilegias are "not difficult to grow in conditions appropriate for a choice *Aquilegia*," makes me slightly crazy: all my attempts so far have resulted in humiliating failure.

My understanding is that a monograph, or some other treatment, of the genus *Paraquilegia* has been published in Czech (or one of the many other languages incomprehensible to me). Why any person who cherishes sanity would want to tackle this subject is beyond me. Perspicacious rock gardeners wanting seed of these species will do well to search the various private seed lists drawn up as a result of expeditions to the remote—and potentially dangerous—locations that are the haunts of paraquilegias.

Paraquilegia anemonoides (Willdenow) Ulbrich (Plate 53), found in rock crevices at elevations sometimes exceeding 3,500 meters, is a glabrous cushion plant about 30 mm high, reportedly growing to an impressive, yet never precisely delineated, width in the wild (a width doubtless rarely equaled in cultivation) with biternate green leaves, flowering stems about 80 mm high, and 20-mm-wide purple or bluish flowers, the elliptic-ovate sepals about 12 mm long. The seeds are wrinkled on the surface (visible with a 20× lens), which is the most diagnostic feature. *Paraquilegia anemonoides* is sometimes available from nurseries specializing in rock garden plants, and sometimes available as seed, usually under the name *P. grandiflora*. Various color forms are doubtfully available in the trade.

The synonyms associated with *Paraquilegia anemonoides* are an absolutely harrowing example of the imprecision of botany and the fallibility of observation, with more than a touch of opera buffa thrown in. Originally described as *Aquilegia anemonoides* by Willdenow in 1816, it then became *Isopyrum grandiflorum* Fischer ex DC. in the *Prodromus* of 1824; then, in the fatally erroneous view of some authors, it became *I. uniflorum* in 1875. Drummond and Hutchinson (1920) semi-successfully transferred Willdenow's taxon to *Paraquilegia*, but they used Fischer's specific epithet *grandiflorum* instead of the perfectly valid, and earlier, *anemonoides*. They then used Karelin and Kirilov's 1842 *Isopyrum anemonoides* as a starting point from which to leap to *I. uniflorum*, renaming it *Paraquilegia uniflora*. The *Flora of the U.S.S.R.* compounded the problem by changing Drummond and Hutchinson's *P. uniflora* to *P. anemonoides*, expropriating Karelin and Kirilov's name and even creating a section Isopyroides for what was, in fact, the wrong species in the wrong genus.

Paraquilegia grandiflora, then, is properly *P. anemonoides*; and the species that suffered name after name attached to it, Karelin and Kirilov's *Isopyrum anemonoides*, is just that, *I. anemonoides*.

Paraquilegia microphylla ("small-leaved") is similar to *P. anemonoides* but has smaller, glabrous biternate leaves with deeply cut lobes. The flowering stems are 30 to 150 mm tall, the elliptic-obovate sepals are 15 to 25 mm long. According to Polunin and Stainton (1997), plants in the western Himalayas have smaller, white flowers (closer in size to those of *P. anemonoides*), while those in the eastern Himalayas have much larger lilac-colored flowers. The seeds are smooth on the surface.

Paraquilegia caespitosa ("tufted," referring to the plant's habit) is similar to both *P. anemonoides* and *P. microphylla*, but the basal leaves are ternate, and the entire plant is densely glandular-puberulent. The flowering stems are 4 to 6 cm tall. The flowers are slightly larger than those of *P. anemonoides*, the oblong sepals 10 to 12 mm long, reddish purple to almost pink; the seeds are wrinkled on the surface.

Paraquilegia altimurana, described in *Flora Iranica* from the Altimur Pass in northeastern Afghanistan, is lightly hairy throughout, the flowering stems 20 to 30 mm high, the oblong-obovate sepals are about 8 mm long, the flowers are white.

Paraquilegia chionophila ("snow-lover"), said to be from near Kabul, is thought by some to be an isopyrum.

Readers who may by now be thinking that almost everything is thought by some to be an isopyrum will doubtless be amused at the idea that the previously-thought-to-be-deceased *Paraquilegia uniflora* was resurrected by Rechinger in *Flora Iranica* in order to name a species with no cauline leaves and flowers with sepals 7 to 8 mm long, endemic to the Safed Kuh in northern Pakistan. Rechinger's plant harks back to the old *Isopyrum uniflorum*, but he recognized only the type of this species (Aitchison 802, collected in the Shendtoi Valley in the Safed Kuh in Pakistan in 1879) as *P. uniflora*.

At least one other species has been named, *Paraquilegia scabrifolia*. Its status is also uncertain. According to *Flora Iranica*, two other paraquilegias, *P. kareliniana* and *P. afghanica*, are actually synonymous with our old friend *Isopyrum anemonoides*.

Seed of these plants often takes two years or more to germinate (I have experience with this aspect), so if you happen to acquire some, it would be advisable to keep the seed pots in a protected location outdoors, and be patient. The seedlings are incredibly small and look exactly like columbines dancing on the head of a pin.

CHAPTER 8

The Species

❦

T HE PRINCIPAL authority in the genus *Aquilegia*, Philip A. Munz, recognized sixty-seven species in his 1946 monograph. Munz tended to
be a "splitter," inclined to recognize even the slightest variation in flower
shape as a distinct entity; as a result, his monograph, a staggering achieve-
ment by any standard, is strewn with a proliferation of subspecies and
varieties. In the years since Munz's work, many of the subspecies and
varieties recognized by him have been discarded in favor of a more generalized approach to the concepts of species, subspecies, and variety, and
a number of names have moved back and forth between species and subspecies depending on the individual perspective of the botanist. No treatment since has had the scope of Munz's work. The largest treatments have
been those in *Flora Europaea* (Cullen et al. 1993) and *Flora of North America* (Whittemore 1997); the rest have been more narrowly regional. The
impression one gets from the various treatments published since Munz's
work is a scant regard for consensus.

   In this chapter I have attempted a synthesis of the often-contradic-
tory statements in all, or almost all, the available literature. I have drawn
heavily on the information supplied in Munz's monograph, and compared it with other information; the quotations from Farrer are from *The
English Rock-Garden* except where noted. All other quotations, except
where noted, are from Munz. I have resisted the temptation of including
my own conclusions in some instances since my primary aim is to en-
courage gardeners to look more closely at the plants in their gardens and
not be so enamored of the names on the labels.

It is strange that in a genus as popular as *Aquilegia* so many species are essentially nonexistent in horticulture. Many of them have been known for almost 150 years, but they exist only in the scientific literature, where they are described with little elucidating comment; and probably about half of these exist only as specimens in various herbaria throughout the world. In horticulture they are relegated to the footnotes reserved for plants of botanical interest only. The European species *Aquilegia grata*, *A. kitaibelii*, *A. thalictrifolia*, and *A. transsilvanica*, all known for more than a hundred years, can hardly be said to have stimulated the imagination of horticulturists. There seems to be no good reason for this; the neglect of the Siberian *A. glandulosa* (at least in this country), known to science since 1822, is perhaps most baffling of all.

The obscurity under which many species have fallen may be attributed to the usual political tensions. It is perhaps understandable that species like *Aquilegia amurensis*, *A. borodinii*, and *A. colchica*, all Russian species described in the 1920s and '30s by Soviet botanists, never had much chance of entering cultivation. With changing political situations, the horticultural status of at least some of these columbines may change as well.

The shifting political climate affects all countries, and it is now, unfortunately, virtually impossible to import columbine seed and plants into the United States. As of 15 January 2002, all imports into the United States require a phytosanitary certificate attesting that the plants will not prove invasive (i.e., escape out of cultivation). This is a very difficult thing to demonstrate either way, but the burden of proof is on the exporter. As a result it is safe to say that most columbine seed will now never reach this country. To my knowledge, no other country has such a restrictive view of non-native plants; U.S. gardeners who want to grow every known species of columbine will probably be forced to become expatriates, or at least acquire an additional garden in some other country.

It is frustrating, to say the least, to be writing about, and recommending, plants that gardeners in my country will now have little chance to grow. We can only hope that government officials will come to their senses some day, or that U.S. citizens will be able to exert enough pressure on elected officials to have these restrictive regulations rescinded.

The genus has been subjected to a few attempts to organize it into various sections and subsections; some taxonomic treatments in individual floras still follow these usages. The earliest attempt, perhaps, and in some ways the most elegantly simple, was made by Parkinson in his *Paradisi in Sole Paradisus Terrestris* (1629); he divided the columbines into five horticultural groups: the "single colombines" ("Aquilegia vulgaris flore simplici"), all the columbines with single flowers, thus encompassing all species, known and unknown; "double colombines" ("Aquilegia vulgaris flore pleno") with "very thicke and double flowers"; the "double inverted colombines" ("Aquilegia inversis corniculis"), the difference between these and the preceding being the flowers, "the heeles or hornes of these are turned inward, and stand out in the middle of the flowers together"; the "rose colombines" ("Aquilegia rosea"), spurless flowers with multiple sepals; and last, the "degenerate colombines" ("Aquilegia degener"), encompassing various mutants with the outermost row of sepals greenish or purple green. The degenerate columbines are discussed in the chapter on hybrids.

Baker, writing in the *Gardeners' Chronicle* in 1878, divided columbines into three horticultural groups, the distinctions made by Parkinson having become moot (many of the more unusual variants had fallen from favor over the years). Baker's divisions were based on flower size: small-flowered (Micranthae), medium-flowered (Mesanthae), and large-flowered (Macranthae). Life should be so easy.

In 1882 the Hungarian botanist Vincze tól Borbás divided *Aquilegia* into two groups, still based on flower shape: the Subscaposae, small plants with mostly basal leaves, and Elatiores, larger plants. These two divisions were then further subdivided: Subscaposae into Orthcentrae (with straight spurs) and Campylocentrae (with curved spurs), with further divisions still; and Elatiores into Brevicornes (spurs shorter than blades), Vulgares (spurs not shorter than blades, flowers as long as they are wide), and Longicornes (flowers much longer than wide). Munz noted that this system required unnatural dissociations between similar species.

Payson (1918) divided *Aquilegia* into what he thought were "three quite distinct sections," which might be glossed over quickly as Cyrtoplectrae ("small blue or white nodding flowers"), Rhodanthae (larger flowers, mostly red, but sometimes yellow), and Macroplectrae ("large, erect, blue, white or yellow flowers"). The divisions included more refining characteristics, of course.

Bulavkina (1937) employed his own divisions, or series as they were called: Parviflorae (small-flowered), Leptocerates ("low-growing glabrous or glabrate plants with slender straight or arcuately declinate spurs"), Orthocerates (nodding flowers with slender spurs and exserted staminodes), Vulgares (species like *Aquilegia vulgaris*, essentially), Glandulosae (large-flowered plants with short spurs), Sibiricae (plants with glaucous leaves), and Colchicae ("glandular-glutinous" plants with hooked spurs). Again, there were many more characteristics to each group.

Grant (1952) proposed yet another way to divide the genus, this time into five complexes based on pollination mechanisms and geography. The first, based on *Aquilegia ecalcarata*, is a complex with a single spurless species. The second, the *A. vulgaris* complex, contains all species with hooked spurs in Eurasia and North America. The *A. alpina* complex contains all species with straight, or at least not hooked, spurs; the *A. canadensis* complex contains all species with nodding red flowers, ones obviously pollinated by hummingbirds; and the *A. coerulea* complex, suberect to erect flowers with straight spurs and blue, yellow, white, or pink flowers. The tendency of some species like *A. parviflora* and *A. nivalis* to lack spurs creates some trouble with this otherwise elegant arrangement (Grant suggested that these represented forms transitional with the alpina and vulgaris groups).

Taylor (1967) expanded Grant's vision to eight complexes, adding Viridiflora (separated out of the alpina group for its disinclination to cross with that species), Brevistyla (effectively a species partly of the Old World because of its hooked spurs, and partly of the New World because of the readiness with which it crosses with straight-spurred North American species), and Flabellata (blue-flowered Asiatic species).

Even with all these attempts to divide the genus, there is no one entirely satisfactory method. They seem to work reasonably well when only a segment of the genus is covered, and each eventually requires that a species be placed in two or more sections. *Flora d'Italia*, for instance, fairly successfully groups the Italian species into *Aquilegia vulgaris* group, *A. alpina* group, and *A. einseleana* group, but even here, a species (*A. litardieri*) with hooked spurs has to be included in the einseleana group, where hooked spurs do not belong.

In the mostly generalized descriptions that follow, it is important to remember that some of the features (presence of hairs, glands, and so forth) can be seen only with a lens of at least 20×, or if the sun strikes the plant in just the right way.

THE KEYS

The keys that follow are divided into Asian, European, and North American species, the creation of keys by continent being a vastly easier undertaking for the person attempting them. Obviously Europe and Asia are one continent, but there is a marked, possibly artificial, discontinuity in the species distribution from Greece to the Caucasus.

Artifice is, in fact, an essential ingredient in any attempt to separate species by individual characteristics. A described characteristic is not necessarily a viable one, as far as making distinctions goes, when viewed over the spectrum of individual plants. Clearly *Aquilegia bertolonii*, for instance, is no more than a regional variant of *A. pyrenaica*, and equally clearly, the various yellow-flowered aquilegias in the southwestern United States are probably nothing more than variants of a polymorphic *A. chrysantha*; but I have not attempted to synthesize any of the species into more broadly defined single species.

The keys follow fairly arbitrary lines of distinction. I have adapted the fine example of Whittemore (1997) in *Flora of North America* to my own ends; the Asian key is entirely of my own design, as is the European key, which may be considered a monument to despair. Several species have varying characteristics that allow them to appear more than once in a key, but in Europe more than perhaps anywhere else, the species bear a closer resemblance to each other.

Not all species are included in the keys. Those for which I have no complete Latin description are absent; perhaps some time in the future these will be more thoroughly understood, and their relative positions in the genus will become clear.

Key to the Asian species of *Aquilegia*

1. Spurs lacking, saccate, or, if present, then less than 10 mm long and not hooked 2
1. Spurs present, greater than 10 mm long 4

2. Spurs entirely lacking, or saccate, sepals 12 to 15 mm long . . . . A. ecalcarata
2. Spurs less than 10 mm long, rarely saccate; if saccate, then sepals 22 to 30 mm long 3

3. Stems glabrous, sepals less than 20 mm long, stamens exserted . . . . A. parviflora
3. Stems densely pubescent, sepals greater than 20 mm long, stamens included . . . . A. nivalis

4. (1) Spurs hooked at tips 5
4. Spurs straight, curving inward, or basally coiled, but never hooked 15

5. Basal leaves usually ternate 6
5. Basal leaves usually biternate 8

6. Cauline leaves present, sepals divergent, flowers nodding . . . . A. flabellata
6. Cauline leaves absent 7

7. Stems glabrous, sepals obtuse, flowers nodding . . . . A. sibirica
7. Stems glabrous below, glandular-pubescent above, sepals acute, flowers suberect . . . . A. amurensis

8. (5) Sepals spreading 9
8. Sepals divergent 12

9. Sepals spreading, not divergent, greater than 20 mm wide . . . . A. glandulosa
9. Sepals spreading, not divergent, less than 20 mm wide 10

10. Sepals acute, lanceolate-ovate, spurs 10 mm long . . . . . A. karelinii
10. Sepals long-acuminate or subacuminate, not acute 11

11. Sepals long-acuminate, stems pilose . . . . A. pubiflora
11. Sepals subacuminate, stems glandular-pilose . . . . A. olympica

12. (8) Stems densely viscid-pubescent . . . . A. colchica
12. Stems subglabrous, sparsely pilose 13

13. Sepals obtuse . . . . A. flabellata
13. Sepals acuminate, not obtuse 14

14. Sepals purple, laminae yellowish . . . . A. oxysepala
14. Sepals concolorous (purple) . . . . A. yabeana

15. (4) Spurs coiled at the base, not hooked . . . . A. incurvata
15. Spurs not coiled at the base, straight, or curving inward,
    not hooked 16

16. Sepals divergent, or at least not spreading 17
16. Sepals spreading 19

17. Sepals divergent, flowers concolorous (purple) . . . . . A. atrovinosa
17. Sepals divergent, flowers bicolored 18

18. Sepals divergent, or slightly so, flowers green, laminae
    reddish brown, purple, or yellowish . . . . A. viridiflora
18. Sepals divergent, purple, 15 to 25 mm long, laminae
    yellowish . . . . A. buergeriana

19. (16) Sepals white, or more or less so 20
19. Sepals not white (blue, lilac, purple, red-purple) 21

20. Sepals 25 to 30 mm long, stamens included or equal to
    laminae . . . . A. fragrans
20. Sepals 15 to 20 mm long, occasionally reflexed, stamens
    exserted . . . . A. lactiflora

21. Basal leaves crowded 22
21. Basal leaves not crowded 23

22. Sepals 15 to 22 mm long, lilac, laminae white . . . . A. borodinii
22. Sepals 13 to 18 mm long, purple, bluish purple . . . .
    . . . . A. moorcroftiana

23. (21) Sepals 20 mm long, purple, spurs 15 mm long . . . .
. . . . A. turczaninovii
23. Sepals 22 to 32 mm long, purple, acuminate, spurs 17 to
20 mm long . . . . A. rockii

Key to the European species of *Aquilegia*

1. Spurs strongly hooked 2
1. Spurs straight, or curving 12

2. Flowers concolorous 3
2. Flowers bicolored 9

3. Flowers yellow . . . . A. aurea
3. Flowers blue, blue-violet, rose, violet-black, or white 4

4. Flowers violet-black 5
4. Flowers blue, blue-violet, rose, or white 6

5. Stems densely pilose above, sepals 15 to 25 mm long . . . . A. atrata
5. Stems glandular-pubescent above, sepals 25 to 35 long . . . .
. . . . A. nigricans

6. Basal leaves ternate, flowers blue-violet, stems sparsely
hairy above . . . . A. litardierei
6. Basal leaves biternate 7

7. Stems glandular-pilose, viscid, flowers blue-violet or white . . . .
. . . . A. viscosa
7. Stems not viscid 8

8. Sepals 22 to 40 mm long, spurs 10 mm long, flowers . . . .
blue-violet . . . . A. transsilvanica
8. Sepals 18 to 25 mm long, spurs 15 to 22 mm long . . . . . A. vulgaris

9. Sepals 25 to 30 mm long, blue, basal leaves ternate, stems
not glandular-hairy . . . . A. dinarica
9. Sepals less than 25 mm long, basal leaves biternate 10

10. Flowers nodding 11
10. Flowers suberect . . . . A. nuragica

11. Sepals 18 mm long, spurs 14 mm long, stems glandular-
    hairy . . . . A. ottonis
11. Sepals 18 to 25 mm long, spurs 15 to 22 mm long (blades
    white in bicolored forms) . . . . A. vulgaris

12. (1) Flowers concolorous 13
12. Flowers bicolored 23

13. Flowers white, nodding, sepals 17 to 24 mm long . . A. barbaricina
13. Flowers blue, pale blue, blue-violet, reddish violet 14

14. Stamens included 15
14. Stamens exserted 21

15. Flowers suberect, stems densely glandular-hairy above . . . .
    . . . . A. kitaibelii
15. Flowers nodding 16

16. Sepals 20 mm long, or less 17
16. Sepals greater than 20 mm long, or, if not, then 9 to 22 mm
    wide 18

17. Basal leaves ternate . . . . A. pyrenaica
17. Basal leaves biternate . . . . A. einseleana

18. Sepals 30 to 45 mm long, stems pubescent above but not
    glandular . . . . A. alpina
18. Stems glandular-pubescent above 19

19. Sepals 25 to 35 mm long, reflexed at tips, flowers pale blue . . . .
    . . . . A. bernardii
19. Sepals not as above 20

20. Basal leaves pilose beneath . . . . A. bertolonii
20. Basal leaves glabrous beneath . . . . A. pyrenaica

21. (14) Plants glandular-pilose throughout . . . . A. grata
21. Plants glandular-pubescent 22

22. Leaflet segments divergent, the center segment elongate ....
.... A. thalictrifolia
22. Leaflet segments not divergent, thick .... A. pyrenaica

23. (12) Basal leaves ternate, stamens included .... A. pyrenaica
23. Basal leaves triternate, stamens exserted .... A. pancicii

Key to the North American species of *Aquilegia*

1. Spurs hooked 2
1. Spurs straight, or curved inward 4

2. Flowering stems longer than basal leaves .... A. brevistyla
2. Flowering stems not longer than basal leaves 3

3. Spurs and sepals blue .... A. saximontana
3. Spurs and sepals white, sometimes tinged with green ....
.... A. laramiensis

4. (1) Spurs and sepals blue, blue-purple, pink, or reddish
   purple, never yellow 5
4. Spurs and sepals red, yellow, pink, or yellowish green 8

5. Leaflets glandular, viscid-pubescent .... A. micrantha
5. Leaflets not glandular 6

6. Spurs to 15 mm long, cushion plants .... A. jonesii
6. Spurs 25 to 75 mm long 7

7. Leaflets crowded, spurs 25 to 40 mm long .... A. scopulorum
7. Leaflets not crowded, spurs 25 to 75 mm long .... A. coerulea

8. (3) Spurs red 9
8. Spurs yellow, pink, or cream 17

9. Sepals yellowish green, never red .... A. skinneri
9. Sepals red 10

10. Sepals spreading or reflexed 11
10. Sepals erect or divergent 14

11. Laminae absent, spur orifice cut at an angle . . . . A. eximia
11. Laminae truncate, or, if not truncate, then less than 6 mm
    long 12

12. Leaflets villous-glandular . . . . A. grahamii
12. Leaflets glaucous 13

13. Leaflets glaucous, especially beneath; basal leaves triternate . . . . . .
    . . . . A. shockleyi
13. Leaflets glaucous, less so beneath; basal leaves biternate . . . .
    . . . . A. formosa

14. (10) Sepals erect, barely exceeding length of laminae . . . .
    . . . . A. elegantula
14. Sepals erect or divergent, exceeding length of laminae 15

15. Basal leaves biternate 16
15. Basal leaves triternate . . . . A. triternata

16. Laminae yellow or yellow-green, leaflets large, to 40 cm;
    plants of eastern North America into Texas . . . . A. canadensis
16. Laminae yellow or yellow-green, leaflets to 30 cm; plants
    of northern Arizona . . . . A. desertorum

17. (8) Spurs greater than 40 mm long 18
17. Spurs 40 mm long or less 20

18. Spurs 90 to 150 mm long, laminae spatulate or spatulate-
    obovate . . . . A. longissima
18. Spurs 40 to 70 mm long 19

19. Sepals 10 mm wide, or less, basal leaves triternate . . A. chrysantha
19. Sepals ca. 17 mm wide, basal leaves biternate . . . . . A. hinckleyana

20. Spurs and sepals yellow, flowers erect or nodding, or, if
    sepals pink, then flowers nodding 21
20. Spurs yellow, cream, or pink, flowers erect to nodding 22

21. Spurs stout, ca. 15 mm long, sepals yellow (pink in var.
    miniana) . . . . A. flavescens
21. Spurs slender, 30 to 40 mm long, sepals yellow . . . . . . A. chaplinei

22. (20) Sepals 20 to 25 mm long, laminae 8 to 14 mm long,
flowers erect . . . . A. pubescens
22. Sepals 10 to 20 mm long, laminae less than 10 mm long 23

23. Leaflets viscid-pubescent . . . . A. micrantha
23. Leaflets not viscid-pubescent . . . . A. barnebyi

DESCRIPTIONS OF THE SPECIES

Aquilegia alpina Linnaeus
in Sp. Pl. 533 (1753)

Aquilegia alpina (Plate 9) is a relatively rare inhabitant of subalpine meadows (in German, *Alp* refers to these high meadows) in southwestern Switzerland, Austria, and northwestern Italy. The type locality is given simply as "Helvetia" (Switzerland). Elsewhere, this "glorious wonder of the lower alpine copse" is somewhat less rare, such as in the Maritime Alps in France, where "all the rolling woods are waving-blue with the acres of its blossom, floating down the distances in a haze of dreamy peat-reek like bluebells in an English May" (Farrer). Even Munz almost broke down completely, writing, "It is one of the most beautiful of all Aquilegias."

In its natural habitat, *Aquilegia alpina* favors moist, calcareous soils (the peat-reek notwithstanding), growing in the open meadows or among shrubs. It grows 15 to 60 cm high or so, with biternate basal leaves. The leaflets are thin, membranaceous, deeply and multiply lobed, glabrous above and somewhat glaucous below. The stems are pilose below, densely pubescent above, with one to three cauline leaves gradually becoming smaller in the upper parts of the stem. The flowers are nodding, blue in almost all parts, with long (30 to 45 mm), oblanceolate, widely spreading sepals, greenish white at the tips (like so many other species). The blades are oblong, almost straight in appearance, 14 to 17 mm long, but slightly curved outward at the ends. The stout spurs, 18 to 25 mm long, are either straight or incurved at the tips, sometimes strongly incurved, but not quite hooked. The stamens are included.

Aquilegia alpina would scarcely be accepted into the genus if it did not have at least a couple of varietal names attached to it at one time or another; a relatively smaller form, to 30 cm, with much smaller flowers, was at one time called var. *minor*, and an even smaller plant, to 20 cm, was called forma *gracilis*. Neither of these names has survived the vagaries of aquilegia taxonomy. However, a cultivar called 'Blue Berry' (Plate 12) is occasionally available; this is said to be a very dwarf plant with nodding or somewhat erect blue flowers. Some authorities consider this a dwarf version of *A. bertolonii*; the plant I grew under this name looked very much like a dwarf version of *A. alpina* but with suspiciously thicker leaflets than any self-respecting *A. alpina* ought to have. In fact I received this plant under the name *A. alpina* and attach the suggested name of 'Blue Berry' to it only with much reluctance.

Most plants offered in the trade as *Aquilegia alpina* are impostors; a pity, too, as Farrer said (when he was dealing with *Aquilegia* species beginning with the letter A), "There can be nothing more beautiful in all nature." As with many columbines, the genetic purity seems to have been diluted by cultivation through the centuries, so that nowadays most plants labeled *A. alpina* are really hybrids of *A. vulgaris* (strongly hooked spurs may be considered a dead giveaway). A few horticultural varieties were in the trade in the early part of the twentieth century, among them (to write their names in currently accepted practice) 'Alba', 'Atrocaerulea', 'Atroviolacea', 'Caerulea', 'Grandiflora', and 'Superba'. Munz notes that trials of these "varieties" at Wisley in 1927 showed some of them to be of "mixed stock"—in other words, of dubious ancestry. In any case, it would be safe to say that genuine color forms of *A. alpina* are now rare to nonexistent, at least in the United States.

Philippe Robert's gorgeous watercolor of *Aquilegia alpina* in Correvon's *Alpine Flora* shows a plant with white blades; the literature does not record such a color combination in the wild, which is another pity. (It does, however, conform with the photograph of *A. alpina* "superba" in Mansfield 1942.) Perhaps life should imitate art more often.

Aquilegia amurensis Komarov
in Not. Syst. Herb. Hort. Bot. U.S.S.R. 6:8 (1926)

Aquilegia amurensis is a species rarely, if ever, encountered in cultivation. Native to areas around the Amur River (eastern Siberia; also reported from northern Korea), the collector and the type locality are given in Munz as "R. Lagar, near Radde, Amur, Siberia." *Aquilegia amurensis* grows to 50 cm, with ternate basal leaves, the leaflets glabrous above and softly downy beneath. There are few if any stem leaves, the suberect flowers have blue-violet spurs and sepals, and whitish, or white-tipped, blades. The spurs are strongly hooked, 10 to 15 mm long, the sepals are elliptical, curving to an acute point, 15 to 25 mm long, and spreading somewhat with respect to the floral axis. The blades are oblong, 7 to 12 mm long, and the stamens are exserted.

Aquilegia amurensis was first described as *A. flabellata* var. *alpina*; it can be distinguished from *A. flabellata* by its suberect, rather than nodding, flowers, and acute sepals. A white form is sometimes given the name *A. amurensis* var. *albiflora*.

There is a fine photograph of *Aquilegia amurensis* in Roy Lancaster's *Travels in China: A Plantsman's Paradise*, on page 455, in which the acute-tipped sepals are clearly visible, although the flowers are more nodding than one would expect from the descriptions in Munz and the *Flora of the U.S.S.R.* Lancaster was traveling at the time in the Changba Shan, which my map tells me is just on the Chinese side of the border of North Korea and China, yet I find no reference whatsoever to this species in the new *Flora of China*. Could *A. amurensis* really be just another variant of the ubiquitous *A. flabellata*? It is another of the unsolved mysteries of the world's columbines.

Aquilegia atrata Koch
in Flora 13:119 (1830)

Aquilegia atrata ("black") is a vulgaris-type, with flowering stems to 60 cm or taller, found on calcareous soils in open woodland and forests from southern Germany south into Austria, Slovenia, and westward into Italy,

France, and Switzerland. The type locality is Wildbad Kreuth on the German-Austrian border. The basal leaves are biternate; the leaflets are glabrous above and glaucous beneath. The stems are more or less glabrous below and densely pilose above. The flowers are all of one color, dark purple-violet, almost black (Munz says "mostly dark purple-violet," but fails to explain the "mostly"), nodding, smaller than those of *A. vulgaris*, with spreading, lanceolate-ovate, acute sepals, 15 to 25 mm long. The blades are oblong, 8 to 12 mm long. The spurs are stout and strongly hooked, 10 to 15 mm long. The stamens are conspicuously exserted.

Like a number of other European columbines, *Aquilegia atrata* is a plant of many names. Farrer confused it with *A. nigricans*, but perhaps excusably so, since Reichenbach had given it this name in 1832, unaware of the earlier use of the name *A. nigricans* by Baumgartner. The species also moved in and out of *A. vulgaris*'s orbit during the nineteenth century, appearing variously as *A. vulgaris* subsp. *atrata*, *A. vulgaris* var. *atroviolacea*, *A. vulgaris* var. *nigricans*, and so on. Farrer's plant with "smaller flowers of a dense chocolate darkness" sounds like our *A. atrata*, while his species "with better blossoms, larger and not so sombre" sounds like *A. nigricans*.

A few varieties, whose names are unfashionable in modern texts, are worth noting if only for their peculiar attributes. *Aquilegia atrata* var. *cyanescens* was Munz's name for a couple of specimens from the Tyrol and Vorarlberg with dark blue flowers and densely glandular-pubescent pedicels. *Aquilegia atrata* var. *salvatoriana*, a variety with "spurs bent backwards," according to Munz, who created this combination, is from Mount San Salvatore in southern Switzerland (the name *salvatoriana* was first given to a variety of *A. vulgaris* by Chevenard in 1905, a combination upheld in *Flora d'Italia*). No one ever postulated the effect of plants being close to hiking trails after contemplating the arrangement of the spurs in this variety; in any case, the name has long since disappeared. A spurless form was once called *A. atrata* var. *nigellastrum*, and plants from the Lech River in Switzerland whose leaflets were pubescent on the underside have been called *A. atrata* var. *major*.

Aquilegia atrata, plain and simple, is a striking plant, occasionally available in the trade (even less occasionally correctly identified) and easily grown. If not particularly long-lived, it is at least freely seeding. A well-known putative color form of *Aquilegia vulgaris*, 'William Guiness', also traveling under the name 'Magpie', has, except for the white-tipped blades, the very color of *A. atrata*. Like many other named varieties of columbines, it is not unreasonable to assume that the attribution of 'William Guiness' purely to *A. vulgaris* is erroneous, and that it really can be counted among the proud—and probably more numerous than anyone suspects—hybrid children of *A. vulgaris* and *A. atrata*.

A natural hybrid of *Aquilegia atrata* and *A. alpina* is sometimes called *A. ×cottia*.

Aquilegia atrovinosa Popov ex Gamajunova
in Bot. Mater. Gerb. Inst. Bot. Akad. Nauk Kazakhsk.
S.S.R. 2:12 (1964)

Aquilegia atrovinosa (Plate 10), a species from Kazakhstan and neighboring provinces in China, is described as growing 30 to 60 cm tall, with a few biternate, slightly pubescent basal leaves. The flowers are dark purple throughout (the specific epithet may be translated as "dark wine-colored"); the sepals are divergent, 25 mm long, the blades about 1 cm long, the spurs are incurved at the base and 15 mm long. *Aquilegia atrovinosa* is probably not in cultivation, although some seed has been available in private seed lists.

Aquilegia aurea Janka
in Österr, Bot. Zeitschr. 22:174 (1872)

Aquilegia aurea ("golden"), the only yellow columbine native to the Old World, is found in woods and in alpine regions in the mountains of Macedonia and western Bulgaria (the type locality is given as "Mt. Perimdagh" in eastern Macedonia), also possibly in Greece (Strid 1986). The plant is more or less glabrous or slightly hairy, with biternate basal leaves, the leaflets glabrous above and downy-glaucous beneath. The flowering stems are 10 to 40 cm high. The relatively large flowers are suberect, rich yellow, with spreading obovate sepals, 20 to 30 mm long, somewhat round at the tips, and oblong blades, 15 to 29 mm long. The stamens are included. The spurs are stout, 15 mm long, and strongly hooked, making this species easily (although one nineteenth-century American botanist thought it a variety of *A. chrysantha*) distinguished from the North American yellow columbines, and, in fact from any other species in the genus.

Seed is sometimes available from rock garden society seed lists or from collectors traveling in the Balkans. I am growing this species from wild-collected seed, but so far it has not deigned to flower. Munz wrote that "a species with the large yellow flowers and hooked spurs of [*Aquilegia*] *aurea* would be a novelty worth having in the garden," but this remains, all these years later, less a potential novelty than an unfulfilled dream.

Aquilegia barbaricina Arrigoni & Nardi
in Boll. Soc. Sarda Sci. Nat. 16:265 (1977)

Aquilegia barbaricina ("outlandish") from Sardinia, judging from the description in *Flora d'Italia*, sounds like a white version of *A. vulgaris*. The plant grows to 50 cm, with pubescent stems and biternate or ternate basal leaves. The flowers are about 25 mm wide and 35 mm long. The sepals are 17 to 24 mm long, greenish at the tips and often lilac-tinged. The spurs are curved, 11 to 17 mm long, but not hooked (which would immediately distinguish it from *A. vulgaris*); the blades are 12 to 15 mm long. The staminodes are equal to the length of the blades, or slightly included. Known from a single population in Sardinia.

Aquilegia barnebyi Munz
in Leafl. W. Bot. 5:177–178 (1949)

Aquilegia barnebyi is an endemic of oil shales in northwestern Colorado (the type locality is Rio Blanco County) and northeastern Utah, growing in pinyon-juniper and other communities, on cliffs where moisture seeping through the shale is constantly available, or on the dry shale itself. (The oil is held in the shale in a consistency like paraffin; despite claims to the contrary, the shale does not "leak" oil.) The pink, or pale pink, ovate-lanceolate sepals, 10 to 15 mm long, are held at right angles to the flower stem; the blades are pale yellow or pink, 6 to 10 mm long, with pink, straight spurs about 25 mm long, sometimes shorter. The flowers are usually nodding, with conspicuously exserted stamens, like a number of other North American species. The foliage is glaucous, almost blue; the leaflets are glabrous, distinguishing it from the glandular-pubescent *A. micrantha* (although some authorities have speculated that these two species are too closely related to retain the specific distinctions). The basal leaves are bi- or triternately compound. *Aquilegia barnebyi* grows to about 60 cm or taller, depending on whether it grows in sun or in shade.

The occasional reference to the similarity of *Aquilegia barnebyi* to *A. triternata* is based on what must have been an aberrant specimen of *A. elegantula* collected by Osterhout near Glenwood Springs, Colorado; Payson (1918) mentioned this specimen in his original description, but *A. triternata* is a red-flowered columbine from Arizona and New Mexico. The other possibility, of course, was that Osterhout made a mistake in his 1951 description of the collected specimen's location.

Despite its provenance, *Aquilegia barnebyi* is an easy plant for the rock garden. No applications of petroleum are necessary for flowering; my plants have lived for many years grown in full sun in an only occasionally irrigated, clay-based dryland rock garden, where the flowering stems reach perhaps 30 cm. Occasionally available from mail-order nurseries.

Named after Rupert Barneby, the twentieth century's foremost authority on the Fabaceae.

Aquilegia bernardii Grenier & Godron
in Fl. Fr. 1:45 (1847)

Aquilegia bernardii, named, according to *Flora d'Italia*, for a French magistrate who studied the Corsican flora, is one of the larger columbines, from the mountains of Corsica. The flowering stems reach 80 cm, the basal leaves are biternate and more or less glabrous. The stems and inflorescence are glandular-pubescent. The flowers are nodding (or suberect according to some authors) "of a most splendid and penetrating soft clear blue" (Farrer), with large, spreading obovate sepals, 20 to 35 mm long, recurved at the tips. The blades are oblong, 15 to 20 mm long. The spurs are slender, 15 to 17 mm long, usually straight but occasionally just slightly curved. *Aquilegia bernardii* is not in cultivation, at least in North America.

Aquilegia nugorensis is a recently described species from Sardinia, at one time, apparently, thought to be a Sardinian version of *A. bernardii*. It is described as being similar to *A. bernardii* but with smaller flowers, and pubescent throughout.

Aquilegia bertolonii Schott
in Verh. Bot. Zool. Ver. Wien 3:127 (1853)

Aquilegia bertolonii (Plate 11), a prized rock garden plant (even when it is incorrectly identified), is found from the Apennines (the type locality) to the Maritime Alps, and has biternate basal leaves, the leaflets sessile, downy-pubescent on their lower surfaces, with nodding, good-sized blue-violet flowers on stems that grow to 25 cm, or sometimes half that height. The sepals are broad, held almost at right angles to the floral axis, 18 to 33 mm long, 9 to 14 mm wide, acuminate to acute. The blades are oblong, 10 to 14 mm long, the spurs straight, or slightly curved inward, 10 to 14 mm long. The stamens are included. Somewhat larger-flowered plants from the Maritime Alps have been called *A. reuteri*. Boissier described *A. reuteri* in the same year as Schott's description of *A. bertolonii*. Farrer said that *A. reuteri* was like a smaller *A. alpina*, "but the flowers, though smaller than those of *A. alpina*, are magnificent and numerous on the graceful foot-high stems, and of a quite peculiar and entrancing soft clear refulgence, like a jewel, which, at twilight, as the blossoms dance in the gathering dusk against the obscurity of the rough grass, seems to glow and burn with a cold electric flame of blue."

It seems almost superfluous to add that plants or seed labeled either *Aquilegia reuteri* or *A. bertolonii* are worth seeking out.

Both Farrer (who described the spurs of *Aquilegia bertolonii* as "incurved and hooked") and Munz (who stated that the spurs could also be hooked) may be responsible for the proliferation of misidentified plants in the nursery trade. The one thing agreed upon in modern floras covering the distribution of *A. bertolonii* is that the spurs are not hooked. The one thing not agreed upon is that this species is so close to *A. pyrenaica* that it may be difficult to justify its separate existence, should a thorough and unprejudiced treatment of the entire genus be undertaken.

Named for the Italian botanist Antonio Bertoloni.

Aquilegia borodinii Schischkin
in Mélang. Bot. Offerts à Mr. J. Borodin à l'occasion de son jubilé, 305 (1927)

Aquilegia borodinii is an alpine species from the Sayan Mountains in southwestern Siberia, roughly in the area to the west and north of the region formerly known as Tannu Tuva. It is found on rocky slopes at elevations up to 2,500 meters, the flowering stems growing 20 to 40 cm with the pedicels and lower stems pubescent. The basal leaves are biternate and crowded. The flowers are small, nodding, the sepals held almost perpendicular to the floral axis and bluish lilac, 15 to 22 mm long, acute at the tips; the blades are whitish, 8 to 10 mm long, the stamens included. The spurs are curved inward, 15 mm long, presumably the same color as the sepals. The presence of pubescence on the pedicels and included stamens are the simplest ways to distinguish *A. borodinii* from its closest relative, *A. turczaninovii*. This species is probably not in cultivation, except in collectors' gardens.

Aquilegia brevistyla Hooker
in Fl. Bor.-Amer. 1:24 (1829)

Aquilegia brevistyla ("short-styled," referring to the very short styles on the follicles; Plate 13) is the northernmost species of *Aquilegia* in the New World, found from Ontario to Alaska (the type locality is given as "western parts of Canada"), growing on rock outcrops and in meadows, woods, and so forth. There are also disjunct populations in Montana, Wyoming, and South Dakota; "the course of plant history has also brought it to the Black Hills, where it is frequently found on cool, north-facing slopes" (Barr 1983).

The lanceolate sepals are blue, 13 to 16 mm long, acuminate or acute, and held at about a 45-degree angle to the axis of the flower; the blades are off-white, rounded, or flatly rounded, 8 to 10 mm long, with blue, hooked spurs 6 to 7 mm long. The flowers are nodding, with stamens included. The flowering stems may reach 75 cm or higher. The basal leaves are biternately compound; the leaflets glabrous above, glabrous or pilose beneath.

This species is one of three in North America with hooked spurs (the other two are *Aquilegia laramiensis* and *A. saximontana*), which, in the case of *A. brevistyla*, are much shorter than the blades, an evident kinship with the European and Asiatic aquilegias. Looking at the distribution of the three species, it is easy to envision the eastward march of aquilegias across the Bering Strait land bridge into Alaska, and then southward, the species eventually proliferating and losing their hooked spurs as they become more and more subject to the scrutiny of the hummingbird, leaving these three hooked-spurred species as relicts of the original invasion. *Aquilegia brevistyla* is not too common in the trade, but seed is available from specialty sources.

Aquilegia buergeriana Siebold & Zuccarini
in Abh. Akad. Muench. 2:183 (1846)

Aquilegia buergeriana is a Japanese species native to the islands of Honshu, Shikoku, and Kyushu (the type locality was not given in the original description). The flowering stems are sometimes branched, growing 50 to 80 cm high. The stems and pedicels are pubescent; the basal leaves are biternate, the leaflets thick, large (occasionally to 40 mm long and as wide), glabrous above, glaucous beneath. The flowers are good-sized, nodding, the lanceolate sepals are spreading, 15 to 25 mm long, yellowish to brownish wine-purple. The blades are yellow, 10 to 15 mm long, almost truncate, the spurs are usually purplish, 15 mm long, and slightly curved or slightly divergent. The stamens are included. The purple-sepaled forms, which are the ones you are most likely to come across, are strikingly beautiful plants.

All-yellow forms of *Aquilegia buergeriana* have been reported; these are sometimes called forma *flavescens*. Clay (1937) described *A. buergeriana* as a "stronger-growing, taller plant [than *A. akitensis*], with small bicoloured flowers varying in tones, but generally pale yellowish with purple- or brown-tipped, or flushed with uniformly coloured sepals"— which makes me wonder what plant he was contemplating as he wrote. Possibly the only specimen he had seen was a wan plant sucked dry by aphids.

Aquilegia buergeriana var. *oxysepala*, which used to be plain old *A. oxysepala*, is now *A. oxysepala* again, but now shorn of the varieties it had when it was *A. oxysepala* the first time . . . if this makes sense.

Unfortunately, *Aquilegia buergeriana* is a favored food of aphids, at least in my garden, where carelessness often reigns.

Named for F. Buerger, a botanist and collector of Japanese plants.

Aquilegia canadensis Linnaeus
in Sp. Pl. 533 (1753)

Aquilegia canadensis (Plate 15) is the only columbine native to eastern North America, growing in woods and among rocks from approximately the 100th meridian eastward, into southern Canada, but rarely in the Gulf Coast states, with a disjunct population in central Texas on the Edwards Plateau. The type locality is given as "habitat in Virginia, Canada," Canada being the name botanists fell back on when at a loss to describe some place in North America. The typical plant may grow as high as 70 cm, with biternately compound basal leaves. The leaflets are glabrous above, glaucous and more or less glabrous or pilose beneath. The flowers are nodding, the sepals are ovate, red, 10 to 14 mm long, held at a 60-degree angle from the stem; the blades are pale yellow, 6 to 8 mm long, truncate, rounded at the edges. The spurs are red, 20 to 25 mm long, and stout. The stamens are exserted about 10 mm. The impression is of a rather narrow and "pinched" flower, more spur than actual flower.

Any red-and-yellow-flowered columbine you may find growing wild in the East will be this species. Easily obtainable in the trade, and a beautiful plant for the woodland garden, if protected from aphids. Barr wrote

(I find this difficult to believe) that his plants of *Aquilegia canadensis* showed more dependable drought-tolerance than any other species he had grown in his garden. Munz noted that "seed offered by a South Dakota firm [Barr's Prairie Gem Ranch] under the name *A. latiuscula* and said to produce plants 6 dm [60 cm] high are probably *A. canadensis* var. *hybrida*"; Barr called his plants *A. latiuscula*, which does occur in Nebraska, where he probably collected his seeds. The true identity of Barr's drought-tolerant columbine remains a mystery, and his columbine is now nowhere to be found in the trade.

Munz recognized four other varieties, or as he put it, "geographical variants." These are *Aquilegia canadensis* var. *coccinea*, essentially larger than the typical *A. canadensis*, with stout spurs and oblong sepals, found throughout the range of the species, the type locality being "banks of the Roanoke, Virginia"; var. *hybrida* (possibly, as Munz suggested, hybrids with *A. brevistyla*), like the type but with "coarse" spurs, found from "Manitoba and Minnesota to northern Nebraska" (type locality "among the Rocky Mountains between latitudes 52° and 53°"—which, in the custom of many nineteenth-century descriptions of type localities, is both meaningless and geographically wrong); var. *australis*, the Florida version (type locality "Marianna, Walton County, Florida") with triternate basal leaves; and var. *latiuscula* (type locality "rocky woods, Riley County, Kansas"), found south of the range of var. *hybrida*, with triternate basal leaves and slender spurs. All these varieties are now fortunately subsumed under *A. canadensis* itself.

Munz also described several color forms that at least at one time had Latin names attached to them. *Aquilegia canadensis* forma *flaviflora* was an all-yellow-flowered form (but apparently otherwise of normal stature; type locality "high ground west of the Hudson, opposite Poughkeepsie, New York"); forma *phippenii* was salmon-colored (type locality Salem, Massachusetts), forma *albiflora* (type locality near Syracuse, New York) was white. All sound very desirable; why these are not currently in the trade is puzzling.

An extremely attractive dwarf (to 25 cm) selection of *Aquilegia canadensis* with pale yellow flowers is offered under the name 'Corbett'. This was found along an abandoned railbed at Corbett, Maryland, by two young brothers, Andrew and Larry Clemens, and introduced by their neighbor Richard Simon, owner of Bluemount Nurseries in nearby Monkton (Copeland and Armitage 2001). It differs also in its tendency to form compact mounds about as wide as they are high (Perry 1995). Another dwarf variety with the usual red-and-yellow coloration, growing to about the same height, is sometimes called *A. canadensis* var. *nana*, or 'Nana'.

Aquilegia canadensis was widely used by native peoples to cure various ailments and as an aphrodisiac (the crushed seeds were used as perfume). It was also used to "detect bewitchment"; its effectiveness is not stated (Moerman 1998).

Aquilegia chaplinei Standley ex Payson
in Contr. U.S. Natl. Herb. 20:156 (1918)

Aquilegia chaplinei is a dwarf version of *A. chrysantha* endemic to the Guadalupe Mountains of western Texas and adjacent New Mexico (the type locality is actually in New Mexico, at Sitting Bull Falls), growing beside streams and at the base of rocks, or wherever moisture is available in this otherwise very arid environment. Average height is about 40 cm. The basal leaves are delicate, bi- or triternately compound (out of flower the plant looks vaguely like a fern); the leaflets are glabrous and glaucous above and somewhat more glaucous beneath, and occasionally pubescent. The flowers are pale yellow, not quite erect, slightly pubescent, the sepals are lanceolate, acute or blunt at the tips, 13 to 16 mm long, the blades are oblong, truncate, rounded at the edges, 8 to 10 mm long, the spurs 30 to 40 mm long, slender, straight, or slightly spreading. The stamens are exserted about 10 mm or so.

The combination *Aquilegia chrysantha* var. *chaplinei* (Lott 1985) was proposed for a flora of the Chihuahuan Desert, which has yet to appear in print. As a result this species is now sometimes referred to as *A. chrysantha*, although the new name has not found general acceptance, except, it seems, in Texas. Seed is occasionally available, as are plants, particularly from native plant nurseries in the region.

Named for W. R. Chapline, who first collected this species.

Aquilegia chrysantha Gray
in Proc. Amer. Acad. Arts & Sci. 8:621 (1873)

Aquilegia chrysantha ("golden-flowered"; Plate 16) is a robust, beautiful plant, with flowering stems 40 to 120 cm high, usually triternate (sometimes biternate) basal leaves, and large, erect, more or less upward-facing golden-yellow flowers, with exserted stamens. The leaflets are glabrous above and glabrous or slightly pubescent beneath. The sepals are spreading, lanceolate, sometimes slightly ovate, 20 to 35 mm long. The blades are slightly divergent, oblong, rounded at the tips, 8 to 16 mm long; the spurs are spreading, and 40 to 70 mm long. It is difficult to mistake this species for any other in the genus—except, of course, for the other species that some botanists believe to be part of a larger *A. chrysantha* complex.

Aquilegia chrysantha is native to moist places, roughly from the Grand Canyon southward, through New Mexico (the type locality is in the Organ Mountains), the Davis Mountains of western Texas, and into northern Mexico (Sonora and Chihuahua), with an oddly disjunct population in south-central Colorado. The Colorado plants have been called *A. chrysantha* var. *rydbergii*; they are generally smaller-flowered, with sepals 10 to 18 mm long, and spurs 35 to 40 mm long. This variety is not recognized as distinct in the new *Flora of North America*.

Aquilegia chrysantha is said to intergrade with *A. coerulea* var. *pinetorum* north of the Grand Canyon. Munz noted that it was difficult to distinguish between dried herbarium specimens of the two. Both species are pollinated primarily by hawkmoths.

A population of plants growing in the Baboquivari Mountains of southern Arizona, with yellow blades, paler yellow spurs and sepals, and spurs to 10 cm long, is considered by some authorities to be an undescribed variety of *Aquilegia chrysantha*, while others believe it to be a disjunct population of *A. longissima*. Sally Walker of Southwestern Native Seeds, who offers seed of these plants and has spent a considerable amount of time studying them, thinks that they may be a new species. My own impression, having grown plants from seed collected at this location, is that the plants are closer to *A. chrysantha* than to *A. longissima*; the spurs on my plants were only about 60 mm long, which is within the range usually given for *A. chrysantha*, but this could be the result of deficiencies in my growing conditions.

The three other yellow-flowered species (there may actually be more, according to one botanist with whom I corresponded) in North America resembling *Aquilegia chrysantha*, may represent, as suggested earlier, a larger, polymorphic complex in which all three species, namely *A. chaplinei*, *A. hinckleyana*, and *A. longissima*, are varieties of *A. chrysantha*. I have seen no published data to support this. If *A. chrysantha* were to be redefined in a broader sense than previously understood, it would very neatly sew up the loose ends of various yellow-flowered columbines hiding here and there in the southwestern United States, and there would be a definite place to put the Baboquivari Mountain specimens. Another botanist with whom I corresponded, who had studied the yellow-flowered columbines for some time, said he considered them all to be *A. chrysantha*. It certainly makes life a lot simpler to see things that way.

The parent of several garden hybrids, thanks to its large flowers, *Aquilegia chrysantha* has hosted the usual proliferation of horticultural forms as well. Those originating in the nineteenth century bore pseudo-botanical names: 'Alba' was of course white ("an exquisite dream-like variety," Farrer), 'Grandiflora Alba' was a large white (how large was not specified, just large), 'Alba Plena' was a white with doubled blades, and 'Grandiflora Sulphurea', large again, had sepals "deep cream" and blades "creamy yellow" (Munz). Some modern selections of *A. chrysantha* are 'Silver Queen' (white), and 'Yellow Queen' (yellow, incredible though it may seem; Plate 17). Most plants sold as *A. chrysantha* in the trade are actually 'Yellow Queen' or something else quite similar—huge, golden yellow, gloriously beautiful, and very long-lived.

Aquilegia coerulea James
in Account Exped. Pittsburgh 2:15 (1823)

Aquilegia coerulea (Plates 1, 20, and 21) is *the* columbine to most people, even non-gardeners. The typical plant of *A. coerulea* (sometimes spelled *caerulea*; either one means "blue"—the original spelling, *coerulea*, is now the accepted one in botanical texts) grows about 90 cm tall in wooded areas, with biternately compound basal leaves, the leaflets somewhat thin, green and glabrous above and glabrous or pubescent beneath, 20 to 45 mm long. The flowers are erect. The sepals are spreading, variously ovate, acute to obtuse, 20 to 40 mm long, and are of a most beautiful sky-blue, as are the spurs, which may be spreading outward or almost straight, 30 to 45 mm long. The blades are white, sometimes slightly divergent, 15 to 25 mm long. The stamens are included. *Aquilegia coerulea* is native to central and western Colorado (the type locality is given as "on the divide between the Platte and Arkansas [rivers], Colorado"), northern New Mexico, and southern Wyoming, usually in open clearings in forests.

Above timberline the plants tend to be dwarfed, except in flower size. Fine colonies of this species occur near the summit of the old railroad line across Boreas Pass in Colorado, growing about 20 cm high, and according to *A Utah Flora*, plants at high elevation eventually become so dwarfed that where they approach the habitat of *Aquilegia scopulorum*, they eventually turn into that species (Welsh et al. 1987).

Curiously, this plant is always noted as being the state flower of Colorado, even by those who have never seen the state and who never mention other state flowers; it is the only flower protected by law in Colorado. There must be some mystical connotation in the eyes of many; certainly otherwise staid authors have burst out into poetic rapture when describing this species. The authors, or at least one of them, of the earliest New Mexican flora wrote, "The great blossoms, sometimes six inches [15 cm] in diameter, look like bits of fallen sky, and when the plants cover acres of meadow, as they sometimes do, no words can be found to do them justice" (Wooton and Standley 1915). Farrer, who, as we shall see many times, burst into euphuisms at the slightest provocation, was compelled to write, "She is also, however, of a temper aptly typified by her evanescent loveliness; and is almost more satisfactory in many gardens if treated as a biennial (if pure seed can be got), seeing that thus every year one can arrange for the bewildering show of loveliness that the tuft always achieves in its second season, too often after that to disappear pitilessly from a distasteful world."

Like other members of the genus, *Aquilegia coerulea* hybridizes readily with other species; as Farrer cautioned long ago, in order to obtain the true plant it may be necessary to procure wild-collected seed or purchase plants that have been grown from seed collected from the true species. Even here, in its native home, I find that many of the plants sold as the "blue columbine" usually turn out to be red, or pink.

Besides the type, there is one other more or less distinct variety: *Aquilegia coerulea* var. *ochroleuca* (*A. coerulea* var. *albiflora*) with pale cream-colored flowers (occasionally with light blue sepals), otherwise similar to the type in all its parts, found to the west of var. *coerulea* in similar habitat, from northeastern Nevada through central Utah and into southeastern Idaho and western Wyoming. The type locality is given by Hooker (Bot. Mag. sub. t. 5477, 1864) as "Valleys of the Rocky Mountains, toward the southern sources of the Columbia," which is helpful. Payson (1918) believed that this was a more highly evolved variety, since it exhibited a move westward into more arid regions, and that the off-white color was moving toward yellow in order to evolve to red, eventually. That red was the color selected by a higher form of animal life, the hummingbird, was to Payson extremely suggestive of a greater stage of evolution. I hesitate to say that, as with most plants whose color is described as ochroleucous (yellowish white), the flowers are somewhat less exciting than the description suggests, even though *A Utah Flora* calls them "strikingly beautiful."

Another variety, somewhat smaller, growing 30 to 60 mm high, with ternate or biternate basal leaves, pale blue flowers, and yellowish blades 13 to 17 mm long, is sometimes called *Aquilegia coerulea* var. *alpina*, found in the mountains of western Wyoming, growing in the open at high elevations; the type locality is Union Peak in the Wind River Range in Wyoming. This variety, "differing from the [type] species by such slight characters that it is often difficult to decide as to the identity of a particular specimen" (Payson 1918), is not recognized in the latest edition of *Vascular Plants of Wyoming*.

Plants in southern Utah and adjacent Arizona with longer, slender spurs (to 70 mm), light blue, white, or pink sepals, leaflets less than 20 mm long, and occasionally triternately compound basal leaves are sometimes called *Aquilegia coerulea* var. *pinetorum*. The type locality for this variety is Warm Springs Canyon in the Buckskin Mountains of northern Arizona. Intergradations with var. *ochroleuca* and with *A. chrysantha* have been reported by Munz. Whittemore (1997) suggests that this may not be entirely distinct from the typical *A. coerulea*, and this variety is not recognized in *A Utah Flora*.

Plants without spurs, found around Estes Park, Colorado, have been called *Aquilegia coerulea* var. (or forma) *daileyae*.

Horticultural forms of *Aquilegia coerulea* seem mostly to have genetic material of other species mixed into them; this is particularly true, it would seem, of plants with sepals and spurs in shades of red and those with yellow blades. Forms that are possibly pure *A. coerulea* may be available as 'Alba' or 'Albiflora' (both white, of course). The cultivar 'Snow Queen' may also be pure *A. coerulea*; Munz suggested that its triternate leaves point to *A. coerulea* var. *pinetorum*.

Some other varieties that are probably no longer available, or rather, no longer have the older names attached to them, are 'Citrina' (lemon-yellow); 'Cuprea', or 'Copper Queen' (copper-colored sepals and spurs, and yellow blades); and 'Delicatissima', which is either pale yellow verging on rose or just plain pink, and is different from the variety in the hybrid strain *Aquilegia* ×*haylodgensis*.

'Crimson Star' (Plate 22), a gorgeous thing with red spurs and sepals and cream-colored blades, is fortunately still available in the nursery trade. A red *Aquilegia coerulea* may strike some as suspect. Where does the red come from? If it comes from one of the red-flowered columbines, there seems to be no other trace of their influence, such as nodding flowers or stout spurs. Munz said he was unable to investigate the source of genetic material for these named varieties; perhaps it is just as well that we call plants like 'Crimson Star' red-flowered forms of *A. coerulea* and leave it at that.

A 'Rose Queen' is also still available in nurseries; this obviously has rose-colored sepals and spurs, and white blades.

John White tells me he found a mutant spurless form of *Aquilegia coerulea* var. *coerulea* in which the sepals are spread open fully and are about 6 cm long. Photographs of this amazing form, which he provisionally named "Blue Moon," show the flowers looking more like a large-flowered clematis than a columbine.

The seeds of *Aquilegia coerulea* were chewed by the Gosiute to alleviate abdominal pains; the plant was also used for heart ailments (Moerman 1998).

Aquilegia colchica Kemularia-Natadze
in Trav. Inst. Bot. Tiflis 1:113 (1934)

Aquilegia colchica is endemic to calcareous soils in the western Caucasus (western Georgia, ancient Colchis; the type locality is "the Kvirila River gorge"). The author of the treatment of *Aquilegia* in *Flora of the U.S.S.R.* wrote that he had not seen this species (Bulavkina 1937). Munz wrote that he had not seen it. I certainly have not seen it. And yet it is said to exist. It is described as being "tall"; no measurements have been given, but I assume it does not need to be climbed in order to see the flowers. The *Flora of the U.S.S.R.* even omits an illustration. The stems are glandular-pubescent. The basal leaves are biternate and densely pubescent, covered with soft grayish white hairs. The flowers are described by Munz as being 3 to 5 cm in diameter; the sepals are described as blue or dark blue. The blades are white, short, about half the length of the sepals, almost truncate; the spurs are long and strongly hooked, or spirally twisted inward.

A note in the *Flora of the U.S.S.R.* says that the flowers smell like apples. This sounds to me like an exciting species. Garden-collected seed is occasionally listed in various rock garden society seed lists. No sources of wild-collected seed have surfaced. *Aquilegia colchica* is mentioned in an online database in the Czech Republic; possibly the true species is cultivated there, although the description "tall" would seem to conflict with the lower stature rock gardeners consider desirable.

Aquilegia desertorum Cockerell ex Heller
in Muhlenbergia 1:27 (1901)

Aquilegia desertorum ("of deserts"; Plate 23) is found, despite its name, at fairly high elevations, often growing on sunny, rocky slopes, in north-central Arizona, in "northern Navajo County and Coconino County" (Kearney and Peebles 1951; the type locality is Flagstaff, which, at 2,100 meters, is definitely not in the desert). Similar in general appearance to *A. canadensis*, *A. desertorum* has smaller leaflets, the rather glaucous basal leaves usually biternate, the leaflets glabrous above and pilose beneath, with sepals that are somewhat more widely flaring than those of typical *A.*

Plate 1. *Aquilegia coerulea* var. *coerulea* with sphinx moth (*Hyles gallii*).

Plate 2. *Aquilegia flabellata* var. *pumila*.

Plate 3. *Aquilegia formosa* var. *formosa*.

Plate 4. *Aquilegia*
'Goldfinch' with katydid
(*Scudderia furcata*).

Plate 5. *Aquilegia rockii*
with Chinese swallowtail
(*Papilio xuthus*).

Plate 6. *Aquilegia viridiflora*
var. *atropurpurea.*

Plate 7. *Aquilegia vulgaris* var. *vulgaris* with
western black swallowtail (*Papilio bairdii*).

Plate 8. *Aquilegia vulgaris* 'William Guiness'.

canadensis. The plant is about 30 cm high and is glandular-pubescent, especially in the inflorescence. The flowers are nodding. The sepals are elliptic-lanceolate, red, about 10 mm long; the spurs are stout at the base, then abruptly narrowing about halfway to the tips, straight, and red. The blades are yellow, bluntly rounded at the tips, and 5 mm long. The stamens are exserted, 1 cm longer than the blades.

Aquilegia desertorum is frequently confused with its relatives *A. canadensis* and *A. triternata*, particularly the latter. It can be distinguished from *A. canadensis* by the leaflets, which in *A. canadensis* are twice as long (50 mm, roughly, compared to the 25 mm of *A. desertorum*), not to mention that *A. desertorum* is found only in north-central Arizona. *Aquilegia triternata* has triternate basal leaves, sepals to 20 mm long, and blades to 8 mm long, and is found in southern and eastern Arizona, and western New Mexico.

Haunted by its specific epithet, *Aquilegia desertorum* is offered in the nursery trade as a xeric plant, which it is not. Seed is regularly available.

Aquilegia dinarica G. Beck
in Ann. Naturhist. Hofmus. Wien 6:341 (1891)

Aquilegia dinarica is native to Albania north into Bosnia, growing on limestone in the Dinaric Alps. The basal leaves are ternate, and flowering stems growing to 20 cm. The plant is pubescent in the lower half; the leaves are particularly downy. The flowers are nodding, the sepals are bright blue, about 30 mm long, and held almost at right angles to the floral axis. The blades are white, 20 mm long, and rounded at the ends. The spurs are stout, 15 mm long, strongly hooked, and the same bright blue as the sepals. The staminodes are included, or almost so.

This highly desirable species, like a startling number of other European columbines, is not in cultivation, and virtually no information other than that given in the preceding paragraph exists. Munz devotes two sentences to it. That horticulture would neglect anything bright blue is incomprehensible to me. Polunin (1980) even describes the color as "intense blue." That anyone would be reluctant to risk their life trying to collect seed is much more comprehensible, given the troubles that this part of the world has seen for so many years. *Aquilegia dinarica* spent some time as a variety of *A. amaliae*, during the period when the latter was not considered a subspecies of *A. ottonis*.

Aquilegia ecalcarata Maximowicz
in Fl. Tangut. 20 (1889)

Synonyms: *Semiaquilegia ecalcarata* (Maxim.) Sprague & Hutch.; *S. simulatrix* Drumm. & Hutch.

Aquilegia ecalcarata ("spurless") is, believe it or not, a spurless species, with flowering stems 10 to 60 cm. The plant is overall mostly densely pubescent, with biternate, sometimes triternate basal leaves (Munz says the triternate tendency is developed under cultivation), glabrous above, glaucous and lightly pubescent below, and nodding or suberect flowers on thin, wiry stems. The small flowers are usually wine-purple or dark purple, occasionally white, with oblong-elliptic spreading sepals, 12 to 15 mm long, and oblong, blunt blades 10 to 15 mm long. The stamens are included. Once in a while a plant will have very short or saccate spurs. Native to central and western China at elevations of 3,000 meters or so. The type locality is Amdo Province in eastern Gansu.

Mansfield (1942) said of *Aquilegia ecalcarata* that it was "a shade of colour 'twixt purple and brown, [which] would seem to be repellent but really has a charm quite out of the ordinary."

Being a spurless columbine, *Aquilegia ecalcarata* has had a plentiful number of synonyms assigned it. The plant is common in the nursery trade, usually sold as *Semiaquilegia ecalcarata*, or sometimes as *S. simulatrix*, even though its presence in the genus *Semiaquilegia* was only accepted (if it ever was) for twenty-five years; rarely, if ever, is it sold as an aquilegia. It is a tribute to Carl Ivanovich Maximowicz, perhaps Russia's greatest botanist, that his original perception of this unusual species as an aquilegia is still valid.

Munz considered *Aquilegia ecalcarata* the most primitive species in the genus, a view that has since been disputed. Hodges (1997a), echoing the conclusions of Taylor (1967), suggested instead that the lack of spurs was a secondary characteristic, making this species simply one that lacks fully developed spurs. No doubt if this had been the first species described, the generic name would have been different, and all the rest of the species with spurs would have suffered the indignity of being moved back and forth from one genus to another.

Aquilegia einseleana F. W. Schultz
in Arch. Fl. Fr. Allem. 135 (1848)

Aquilegia einseleana, found on limestone in southern Germany (the type locality is Berchtesgaden in Bavaria), Austria, Slovenia, northeastern Italy, and eastern Switzerland, is rather similar to *A. bertolonii* but with much smaller flowers and less deeply divided leaflets. The foliage is mostly glabrous, the stems being slightly glandular above. *Aquilegia einseleana* is generally taller than *A. bertolonii*, with flowering stems to 40 cm; the basal leaves are usually biternate, and more or less glabrous. The leaflets are sessile, or nearly so, and cut shallowly. The flowers are nodding, blue-purple, with spreading, oblanceolate sepals about 20 mm long. The blades are rounded at the tips, 10 mm long, slightly spreading; the spurs are more or less slender, 10 mm long, and straight, or very slightly incurved at the tips. The stamens are included.

Aquilegia einseleana is yet another European species that can hardly be regarded as being in cultivation. It can be distinguished from *A. bertolonii* by the features just discussed. It is similar to *A. thalictrifolia* but does not have that species' glandular-pubescence; the leaflets are utterly different. Since its discovery, an absurd number of names have been inflicted on this poor species (the name *A. bauhinii* surfaces from time to time), but Schultz's original name, which honored his friend Dr. Einsele, has never been superseded.

Aquilegia elegantula Greene
in Pittonia 4:14 (1899)

Aquilegia elegantula ("somewhat elegant"; Plate 24) is similar in size and appearance to *A. canadensis* and *A. desertorum*. It is found just to the north of the range of the latter, in forests from Utah and western Colorado (the type locality is Slide Rock Canyon in southwestern Colorado) south into New Mexico. In *A. elegantula* the flower has an even more narrow aspect (Munz's term is "subcylindric") than that of *A. canadensis*; the stamens are exserted to about half the length of those in *A. canadensis*. The basal leaves are biternate, glabrous above, glaucous or glabrous below. The sepals are oval-elliptical, erect, barely diverging from the axis created by the flower itself, yellowish at the tips and red nearest the stem, and 7 to 11 mm long. The red, straight spurs, 16 to 20 mm long, are stout at the base then become somewhat pinched, with a bulge at the tip. The blades are yellow, rounded at the tips, and 6 to 8 mm long. The staminodes are exserted about 6 mm from the tips of the blades. The plant grows to about 30 cm, but plants half that size are occasionally available in the trade.

Weber (1987), in his *Colorado Flora: Western Slope*, says that where *Aquilegia elegantula* comes into contact with *A. coerulea*, the two species hybridize, "but because the [resulting hybrid] is most like [*A. coerulea*], the backcrosses are with *A. coerulea*, thereby causing some variability in that species and leaving *A. elegantula* pure," but, according to John White, in a few secluded locations on the Western Slope, the resulting hybrid swarms produce plants with characteristics more recognizably those of *A. elegantula*.

The photograph in Phillips and Rix (1991, page 86) is misidentified, and possibly represents one of the hybrids of *Aquilegia elegantula* and *A. coerulea*.

Aquilegia elegantula has been used as a blood purifier by native peoples (Moerman 1998).

Aquilegia eximia Van Houtte ex Planchon
in Fl. Serres Jard. Eur. 12:13 (1857)

Aquilegia eximia ("exceptional") cannot be mistaken for any other species. This is a larger plant, growing to 90 cm or more, with bi- or triternately compound sharply toothed basal leaves reminiscent of a maple's leaves, densely glandular-pubescent herbage, and nodding red and yellow flowers, without blades. The leaflets are green above and glaucous beneath. The ovate-lanceolate sepals are short, 20 mm or less, and occasionally reflexed with respect to the floral axis. The exceptionally stout spurs are slightly curved at the tips, 18 to 30 mm long, and are cut backward just at the point where they would widen and elongate into blades, giving the flowers a strange, almost mutilated appearance; the flower has the appearance of having only spurs when the blades are fully reflexed. The stamens are exserted, as they would have to be, and are about 20 mm long. *Aquilegia eximia* is native to the California coast ("Mendocino County to San Luis Obispo County, from sea level to higher elevations, frequently in seeps on serpentine"). It is somewhat similar to *A. formosa* var. *truncata*, except in the latter the sepals are much longer and the blades truncate.

Munz has suggested that the lack of blades is not sufficient to distinguish this species from *Aquilegia formosa*, but the reflexed sepals, together with the complete absence of blades, and very stout spurs make *A. eximia* readily identifiable. The absence of blades, like those of *A. formosa* var. *truncata*, is probably an evolutionary adaptation to allow easier pollination by hummingbirds.

Aquilegia flabellata Siebold & Zuccarini
in Abh. Akad. Muench. 2:183 (1846)

Synonyms: *Aquilegia japonica* Nakai & Hara (but see below); *A. fauriei* Lévl. & Vant.; *A. akitensis* Huth.

Aquilegia flabellata ("fan-shaped") is an alpine species found in northern Japan, Sakhalin, and the Kurile Islands. The plant is essentially glaucous, with fairly thick, broad, ternate or biternate basal leaves. The leaflets are more or less fan-shaped, sometimes tinged with purple, glabrous above and glaucous-pilose beneath. The flowering stems grow to about 60 cm, the flowers are nodding, the sepals spreading, elliptic, usually about 20 to 30 mm long, blue or blue-purple, rather rounded or obtuse at the tips. The blades are light purple, rounded, 13 to 16 mm long, light yellow at the tips. The spurs are also light purple, 8 to 20 mm long, and strongly hooked. The staminodes are included. The carpels are glabrous, which is one way to distinguish it from *A. buergeriana*.

The taxonomic and horticultural situation of *Aquilegia flabellata* is peculiarly convoluted. There is a variety, var. *pumila* (Plate 2), which is half the height of the type, somewhat less glaucous, and with more normal-looking (thinner) leaves. The type locality for var. *pumila* is on the beach of the "small island of Rebunshiri," which is to the west of the northern tip of Hokkaido.

The type itself is considered in *Flora of Japan* to have originated from *Aquilegia flabellata* var. *pumila*: "the plant (*A. flabellata* var. *flabellata*) was first described on the basis of the cultivated phase" (Ohwi 1965). If the larger plant was described from a cultivated form of the dwarf plant, it seems to me that var. *pumila* should be the type, and be renamed, to include the larger form as part of a more variable, single taxon. The type is considered synonymous with *A. akitensis* by Ohwi; Munz considers *A. akitensis* to be synonymous with *A. flabellata* var. *pumila*.

There are, or were, several other varieties whose names, thank goodness, have been suppressed by the passage of time. *Aquilegia flabellata* var. *flavida* was a yellow-flowered plant, originally called either *A. japonica* var. *flavida* or *A. akitensis* var. *flavida*; var. (or forma) *globularis* was double-flowered; var. *humiliata* was a cultivated variety with, according to Munz, the "spur curved under the sepals or slightly protruded above them" (it sounds hideous).

Aquilegia flabellata is common in the nursery trade, often appearing under even more confusing names. The cultivar 'Nana' (usually labeled as a botanical variety) is not really different from var. *pumila*; the cultivar 'Nana Alba' (again, usually labeled as a botanical variety, which it is not; Plate 25) is a white form of var. *pumila*. All the plants labeled in the trade as *A. akitensis* (in other words, color forms of *A. flabellata* var. *pumila*) are very beautiful, desirable plants. Plants usually going under the names *A. akitensis* var. *rosea* or *A. flabellata* 'Rosea' (Plate 26) are ravishing dwarfs, as beautiful as any columbine needs to be. Other varieties, such as var. *kurilensis* and var. *sachalinensis*, are sometimes available; these are horticultural varieties with no real botanical standing and are not much different, if at all, from the typical plants.

Aquilegia flabellata has been a favorite of breeders; various color forms of the smaller version of the cultivated form are available in the trade. 'Mini Star' is a well-known selection developed by Benary Seeds of

Germany. 'Maxi Star' is, well, larger. The Cameo series, also Benary's, is similar to 'Mini Star' but blooms two weeks earlier according to advertisements; these are selected color forms, offered in white, blue and white (the blades always being white where two colors are described), blush, pink and white, and rose and white. Mixed colors are also available. These are quite popular as potted plants in the florist's trade.

Curiously, or perhaps not so curiously considering the convoluted taxonomy of this species, the new edition of *Flora of China* gives *Aquilegia flabellata* the name *A. japonica*. With thousands upon thousands of plants already known by what is now a very familiar name, it is likely that the new name will meet with at least some resistance.

Aquilegia flavescens S. Watson
in Botany Fortieth Parallel 10 (1871)

Aquilegia flavescens ("becoming yellow"; Plate 27) is an alpine and subalpine species, growing 20 to 60 cm high, found from British Columbia and Alberta south into western Montana, the Idaho panhandle, western Wyoming, and Utah (the type locality is in the Wasatch Mountains of Utah). The stems are glandular-pilose. The basal leaves are biternately compound, glabrous, glaucous, or glandular-pilose. The flowers are nodding. The sepals are oblanceolate or oblong, elliptical, yellow, or sometimes shades of pink, 12 to 22 mm long, and spreading or reflexed (the latter position seems to be more common). The white or cream-colored blades are relatively long (10 mm) for the flower size and rounded at the tips; the stamens are exserted about 10 mm. The spurs are yellow, 6 to 18 mm long, and slightly curved inward at the tips.

Throughout its range, *Aquilegia flavescens* exhibits practically no self-control when it comes to consorting with other members of its genus. Where it comes into contact with *A. formosa*, intermediates between the two species may be found. Payson (1918), describing a "transitional area" where *A. flavescens* moves westward and develops pink-tinted sepals and straighter spurs, wrote "in the mountains of Custer County, Idaho, the author has seen great patches of a variety with beautiful salmon-colored flowers entirely replacing the red *formosa* and the yellow *flavescens*." The year before, he and Macbride had described a variety, *A. flavescens* var. *miniana* ("painted red"), with pink sepals coming from Challis Creek in Custer County, but he did not acknowledge this variety in his monograph. *Flora of Idaho* (Davis 1952) calls this *A. formosa* var. *flavescens*.

Aquilegia flavescens also forms intermediates with *A. coerulea* in Utah, and possibly with *A. jonesii* in Montana. These putative interminglings with *A. jonesii* are found mostly, if not entirely, within the confines of Glacier National Park in Montana (DeSanto 1991). Their appearance is that of an *A. jonesii* slightly stretched out (the leaflets less crowded); the flowers are shaped like those of *A. flavescens*; the spurs and sepals are the color of *A. jonesii*, the blades rather more yellow than those of typical *A. flavescens*.

Another variety, called *Aquilegia rubicunda* by Tidestrom in Amer. Midland Naturalist 1:168 (1910), with pink spurs and sepals and whitish blades, found in Emery and Sevier counties in Utah (the type locality is "Link Trail" near Emery, Utah), has the smaller flowers and glandular pubescence of *A. micrantha*. According to *A Utah Flora*, it is "allopatric with that taxon [*A. micrantha*], but is contiguous with (if not sympatric with) *A. flavescens*" (Welsh et al. 1987). Still, most treatments, notably that in *Flora of North America*, consider Tidestrom's plant to be a variant of *A. micrantha*.

Aquilegia formosa Fischer ex de Candolle
in Prod. 1:50 (1824)

Aquilegia formosa ("handsome"; Plates 3 and 28) is widespread throughout western North America. The type locality is "Kamchatka." No explanation has ever been offered for this statement; perhaps "Kamchatka" was the equivalent of "somewhere up north" in the early nineteenth century. *Aquilegia formosa* does not grow in Kamchatka according to *Flora of the U.S.S.R.*

Aquilegia formosa is a variable species; generally, the plants grow 50 to 100 cm high, the stems pubescent above, with biternate basal leaves, glabrous or pubescent above, usually pubescent beneath but sometimes glabrous. The sepals are ovate-lanceolate, red, held at right angles to the axis of the flower, or reflexed, and acute or acuminate. The spurs are more or less stout, red, 10 to 20 mm long. The blades are short, rounded (in var. *formosa*), 3 to 6 mm long, and yellow. The stamens are exserted about 10 mm, or slightly more.

The type species is found from southern Alaska (more or less close to Kamchatka) and the Yukon Territory south through British Columbia (and barely sneaking into Alberta) to Idaho, Montana, Utah, and Wyoming, and through Washington and Oregon into northern California and Nevada, in moist areas in forests, woodland, and so forth.

The variability of *Aquilegia formosa* encouraged nineteenth-century botanists to invent a fearsome number of names for the variants, some of which are still recognized in current treatments. Plants with extremely short (less than 2 mm long) or no blades, somewhat reminiscent of *A. eximia*, and with roughly the same aspect, are often called *A. formosa* var. *truncata* (Plate 29). This is a more or less glabrous plant, and the form of *A. formosa* taken in most of California west of the Sierra Nevada; it also appears in western Nevada and southern Oregon; the type locality is Fort Ross in California. *Aquilegia formosa* var. *truncata* can be distinguished from *A. eximia* by its less reflexed sepals, more slender spurs, and the perpendicular cut of the blades. Also, the reflexed sepals of *A. formosa* var. *truncata* appear almost to come out from between the very stout spurs, which in *A. eximia* are cut obliquely backward.

Populations of *Aquilegia formosa* native to woodland in Baja California and extreme southern California (I know this seems incredible— that there could be woodlands remaining in southern California), with viscid-pubescent foliage and the very short blades of var. *truncata*, are *A. formosa* var. *hypolasia*. The type locality for this variety, given by Munz, is "between Campbell's and Cameron's ranches, eastern San Diego County, California." Neither var. *truncata* nor var. *hypolasia* is recognized in the *Jepson Manual*; they are all simply designated *A. formosa*.

Plants with thin leaflets and very pale red flowers are sometimes called *Aquilegia formosa* var. *wawawensis*. This variety, "collected at Wawawai, Washington, on the south bank of the Snake River, 'in dripping water'" (Payson 1918, quoting the discoverer, Rex Hunt), has pale red, ovate-elliptic sepals about 2 cm long; slender, straight or slightly curved spurs about the same length; and yellow blades about 3 mm long. Plants in my garden, grown from wild-collected seed, have sepals and spurs with a distinctly orange cast to them. They grow well without being subjected to dripping water.

It has been suggested that another variety, *Aquilegia formosa* var. *fosteri*, from southwestern Utah (the type locality is Zion Canyon), is part of a hybrid swarm (Whittemore 1997); plants have glandular-pubescent foliage and erect flowers larger than normal for the species.

Aquilegia formosa var. *pauciflora* is a name sometimes given to plants of the "high montane in the Sierra Nevada, observed in its extreme form at Conness Creek and elsewhere in Yosemite Park" (Jepson, quoted in Payson 1918) with scape-like (leafless) stems. Spurless populations in southern Oregon and northern California were at one time called, rather mellifluously, *A. formosa* forma *anomala*. Another name, *A. formosa* var. *kamschatica* (still trying for that connection), was associated with a plant whose flowers had unusually long spurs.

Two subspecies of *Aquilegia formosa* that were at one time thought to be distinct from *A. shockleyi* are discussed with that species.

There also are, or were, a distressing number of horticultural forms saddled with Latin names. 'Rubra Pleno' (or 'Rubra Flore-pleno') has doubled red flowers, 'Rosea Flore-pleno' has doubled rose-colored flowers, 'Nana' is a dwarf with shell-pink flowers, 'Nana Alba' is dwarf with white flowers.

Doubtless because of its considerable geographical range in western North America, *Aquilegia formosa* has been employed in an astonishingly wide variety of uses by native peoples. Moerman (1998) lists about two dozen different uses. Among other things, the roots were used in a decoction as a cough medicine and as an aid for stomachache; the spurs were sucked by children for the sweet nectar; and (my personal favorite), in keeping with the generally dubious reputation of the genus, the plant was used by women as a love charm to attract men.

Aquilegia fragrans Bentham
in Maund, Botanist 4:181 (1840)

Aquilegia fragrans, "a perfectly distinct and lovely plant, unlike anything else in the garden" (Clay 1937, who shared Farrer's propensity for hyperbole), is a variable species native to northern India (the vaguely specified type locality), in Punjab and Kashmir, growing at elevations of 2,500 to 3,500 meters. The plant grows to 80 cm or so, with hairy, occasionally glandular stems. The basal leaves are bi- or triternate, the leaflets are glaucous, glabrous above and slightly pubescent beneath. The flowers are suberect or nodding, sweetly scented, with white or light purple spreading, lanceolate-ovate sepals 25 to 30 mm long. The blades are 15 to 18 mm long and 12 to 14 mm wide, wedge-shaped, truncate, and white or off-white. The short (15 to 18 mm) spurs are also the same color, straight, or slightly curved inward at the tips. The stamens are equal to the blades.

Aquilegia fragrans is occasionally offered in the trade, sometimes as *A. suaveolens* or *A. glauca*. The last two names are now less often used than before, owing no doubt to the salability of plants with the word *fragrans* in their name. The high elevations at which this species is found are no guarantee of hardiness; I have had trouble overwintering it in some years, and this is not a terribly cold climate at this latitude, compared with similar elevations elsewhere in the world. Some gardeners have complained that the flowers smell like cats.

Hybrids of *Aquilegia fragrans* are said to exist in the trade. Where, no one has ever said. Munz said that the fragrance of *A. fragrans* was detectable in these hybrids; at least one person with whom I spoke, who had spent decades breeding columbines, said that the fragrance was the most difficult, if not impossible, characteristic to breed into the offspring between this species and others.

Aquilegia glandulosa Fischer ex Link
in Enum. Hort. Berol. 2:84 (1822)

Aquilegia glandulosa (Plate 30) is a prized rock garden plant by anyone's standards. Farrer, as irredeemably fickle as any gardener, called it "the unquestionable sovereign of the race, annihilating even *A. coerulea* and *A. alpina*." The very large flowers, on a relatively small plant, set it apart from most of the other Asian species. Seed is occasionally available from Czech collectors who venture into the regions where *A. glandulosa* grows, which is how I obtained my seed.

Aquilegia glandulosa is native to alpine and subalpine regions of the Altai Mountains (thought to be the generalized type locality) in western Siberia and also in adjacent Mongolia. Munz says that it occupies roughly the same region as *A. sibirica*, but *A. glandulosa* is the high-elevation species and *A. sibirica* the rather lower one. The plant grows to 60 cm, sometimes to only 10 cm, with glaucous, glandular-pilose stems in its upper parts. The basal leaves are biternate, or mostly so; the almost crowded leaflets are glabrous above and slightly hairy below. The stems are leafless except for a few bracts, which are tiny, in threes below, single above. The flowers are suberect, with large, blue or blue-violet ovate or ovate-elliptic sepals, up to 45 mm long and 25 mm wide, held almost at right angles to the floral axis. The blades are also large, 25 mm long by 15 mm wide, more or less obovate, and blue-purple or white; the spurs are blue-purple, usually shorter than 10 mm, stout, and strongly hooked. The staminodes are glandular-pubescent and included.

The name *Aquilegia glandulosa* has been much confused. Farrer knew the species as *A. jucunda* (he called it, in his panegyrics, "the glorious *A. glandulosa* of our gardens"), thinking, not unreasonably considering the even more massive confusion surrounding columbine names in the early part of the twentieth century (compared to the slightly less massive confusion of the early twenty-first century), that these were two separate species. They are not. The name *A. jucunda* was originally proposed by Fischer in 1840 for what was apparently thought to be a different species; for some reason the plant then became confused with *A. nivalis*, which is indeed a completely different species. For Farrer, *A. jucunda* was the plant some botanists called *A. glandulosa* var. *discolor* (the earliest mention was by de Candolle in his *Prodromus* of 1824), clearly a form with white blades, which he preferred over the "plain" form called, even then, *A. glandulosa*: "The royal flowers are not really horizontally borne, but seem just a little to nod with their own grandeur; and a dense field-like patch of the *A. jucunda*, one foaming sea of green, high over which wave and waver the countless wide stars of blue and white, is one of the most beautiful things that the garden can ever show, either in early June or at any other time." *Aquilegia jucunda* is a synonym for *A. glandulosa*, and as Clay (1937) said, no doubt wearily, "It would avoid confusion if the name *A. jucunda* disappeared completely." If it has not done so, let it do so now.

Aquilegia glandulosa is truly a stunning plant, and, while we may not wish to sweep aside *A. coerulea* and *A. chrysantha* in a beauty contest, it is sad to think how little this plant has been grown, in this country at least. The literature, which comes largely from England (is this surprising?), suggests that cool gardens in Scotland suit it more than the "warmer" southern counties. If I can grow it, there seems to be no reason why others cannot as well.

Aquilegia grahamii Welsh & Goodrich
in Rhodora 95:412 (1993)

Aquilegia grahamii is a newly described species endemic to hanging gardens in Uintah County, Utah, with the glandular herbage of *A. micrantha* but with flowers that are, as the original description puts it, "startlingly red-fuchsia contrasting with yellow," growing to about 50 cm tall, with biternately compound basal leaves, spreading sepals 11 to 14 mm long, and 10-mm-long exserted stamens. The spurs are red, 18 to 21 mm long, and straight; the blades are yellow and 5 to 6 mm long. The plant is described by the authors as having grains of sand stuck to it, making it a debatably attractive addition to any garden where cottonwoods are grown.

"Newly described" does not necessarily mean newly discovered, and, in fact, this species was originally collected in the Uinta Basin in 1935 by E. H. Graham, who thought it was *Aquilegia formosa*, or at least an unnamed variant of it. For almost sixty years, the specimen labeled E. H. Graham 10009 lay in the herbarium, its relationship to the otherwise more westerly distributed *A. formosa* uncontested except for a discreet question mark in *A Utah Flora*. Additional collections in the early 1990s provided enough distinct material to inspire the botanists Welsh and Goodrich to name it a new species in Graham's honor.

Aquilegia grata Zimmeter
in Jahresb. Staats-ober-Realschule Steyr 5:46 (1875)

Aquilegia grata ("pleasant"), from Croatia, Bosnia and Hercegovina, and Serbia, grows anywhere from 15 to 40 cm, with glandular-pilose leaves and stems. The basal leaves are biternate, the flowers nodding to somewhat suberect, red- or purple-violet throughout. The spurs are straight, 15 to 20 mm long, or slightly curved inward; the sepals are ovate, 30 mm long, and recurved at the tips. The blades are 6 to 10 mm long. The stamens are exserted about 4 mm.

For horticultural purposes *Aquilegia grata* may be said to be nonexistent. A few years ago I sowed seeds sent me by the Scottish Rock Garden Club, but the seedlings met with an unfortunate accident one excessively dry and windy day; and so I too know nothing about this plant other than the description just given, which I culled from various texts.

Aquilegia hinckleyana Munz
in Gentes Herb. 7:141 (1946)

Aquilegia hinckleyana, recently proposed as a variety of *A. chrysantha* (Lott 1985), is endemic to a very small area of northwestern Presidio County in Texas. The type locality is Capote Fall on Brite Ranch. This is essentially a smaller version of *A. chrysantha*, growing to 60 cm or so; the not-fully-erect yellow flowers have sepals wider (to 17 mm) than those of *A. chrysantha*. The basal leaves are apparently always biternate and glabrous above, glabrous and somewhat glaucous beneath. The sepals are spreading, ovate, 25 mm long. The blades are more or less spatulate, rounded-truncate, and 20 mm long. The spurs are straight, or incurved at the tips, and about 4 cm long. The stamens are exserted.

Aquilegia hinckleyana seems to be readily available from nurseries, especially those in Texas, where it is usually labeled as a variety of *A. chrysantha*.

Named for L. C. Hinckley, who discovered this species. Lest anyone think that columbines growing in this dry region of Texas could be considered drought-tolerant, Munz's comment is worth quoting: "Mr.

Hinckley reports this as forming a thick bed on the always moist bank under the overhanging cliff at the fall and that he did not find it at any other spot in the Sierra Tierra Vieja."

Aquilegia incurvata P. K. Hsiao
in Ho & Liu, Fl. Tsingling. 1(2):602 (1974)

Aquilegia incurvata, found along streams in central China, is described as growing to 60 cm, with mostly glabrous biternate basal leaves. The small flowers are dark purple, the sepals 14 to 18 mm long, the blades 7 to 8 mm long. The spurs, which are 12 to 15 mm long, are intriguingly described as being coiled at the base. This species is not in cultivation.

Aquilegia jonesii Parry
in Amer. Naturalist 8:211 (1874)

Aquilegia jonesii (Plate 31) is the smallest of all species of *Aquilegia.* Named for Capt. W. A. Jones, who explored northern Wyoming, this cushion-forming (maximum height is about 8 cm) columbine is native to limestone rocks from the Big Horn Mountains of northern Wyoming north to Alberta. The type locality is Phlox Mountain in northern Wyoming. The basal leaves are once- to biternately compound, very densely crowded, and glaucous, often sessile. The plants have no leaves on the stems. The flowers are solitary, erect, purple (occasionally white) and short-spurred (8 to 15 mm long), lacking staminodes, with stamens as long as the blades. The sepals are spreading, oblong-elliptic, and about 20 mm long. Munz thought the absence of staminodes showed a similarity to species in *Paraquilegia,* which *A. jonesii* distinctly resembles in appearance.

Aquilegia jonesii is a highly desirable plant for the rock garden and reportedly difficult to grow, or to flower, in gardens unable to reproduce the conditions it demands: high light intensity, low humidity, heat, and a very limy soil. Few other American alpine plants have inspired so much despairing prose or had so many eulogies devoted to them. Gardeners who have difficulty with this species should try applying a water-soluble

Aquilegia jonesii. Drawing by Carolyn Crawford.

fertilizer sometime in late February. Under suitable garden conditions, which may only exist in the Rocky Mountain region, the plants flower regularly and profusely in March and form cushions about 20 cm wide before finally departing this earth after four or five years. The plants may go dormant in a hot summer; postmortems should be put off until mid-autumn, when tiny new leaves emerging from the base of the plant will signal emergence from dormancy. Absence of these leaves may indicate false dormancy (i.e., death).

A form of *Aquilegia jonesii*, with flowering stems to 20 cm, and occasionally having two flowers (instead of one) to the stem, is sometimes called var. *elatior*; these are generally found in the northern part of the species' range, the type being collected in Glacier National Park in Montana.

Aquilegia karelinii O. & B. Fedtschenko
in Ranunc. Turkestana 65 (1899)

Aquilegia karelinii, named for the Russian botanist G. S. Karelin, is a woodland species, growing 20 to 80 cm high, native to forests—wild-apple forests, among other kinds of vegetation—in the Tien Shan and elsewhere in central Asia (the type locality is the Dzungarian Alatau, a mountain range on the border of China and what is now eastern Kazakhstan) and is quite similar to the much more easterly distributed *A. vulgaris*, with the same nodding flowers and hooked spurs. The stems are glandular-pilose. The basal leaves are biternate, the leaflets glabrous above and lightly hairy beneath. The flowers are violet or wine-colored, and concolorous. The acuminate sepals are widely spreading to reflexed, about 25 mm long; the blades are 9 to 11 mm long, truncate. The spurs are about 1 cm long and strongly hooked. The stamens are barely exserted.

Aquilegia karelinii was, in fact, originally described as a variety of *A. vulgaris* but is now accepted as a valid species. Munz (who called it *A. kareliniana*, thinking there was a legitimate dispute about the priority of the name *karelinii*) said that the principal differences, besides its distribution, were shorter spurs (half the length of those of *A. vulgaris*) and "more pointed staminodia," although, of course, the very short spurs would be the most readily visible distinguishing characteristic. Seed is occasionally available from rock garden society seed lists.

The sap, what of it there is, of the flowers of *Aquilegia karelinii* is said to be used as an ink, when diluted with water, in the "Aulie-Ata region," according to a note in the *Flora of the U.S.S.R.*

Chapter 8

Aquilegia kitaibelii Schott
in Verh. Bot. Zool. Ver. Wien 3:129 (1853)

Aquilegia kitaibelii is yet another in the almost endless list of species found in Croatia and Bosnia and Hercegovina, but almost never found in cultivation. Like most other European columbines, *A. kitaibelii* favors calcareous soils and grows on limestone cliffs. The type locality is given as "Croatia." The stems grow to 30 cm, the basal leaves are biternate, the leaflets sessile, slightly hairy above, densely hairy beneath. The stems are copiously glandular-hairy. The flowers are large, suberect, reddish or bluish violet, with spreading, obtuse sepals (2 cm long, 1 cm wide). The blades are oblong, 10 to 13 mm long. The spurs are short (to 10 mm), and slightly incurved at the tips. The stamens are included.

This species, named for Paul Kitaibel, Hungarian botanist and co-author of a flora of Hungary, has been frequently confused in the literature with the already-completely-confused *Aquilegia viscosa*, which is not found anywhere near the habitats favored by *A. kitaibelii*.

Aquilegia lactiflora Karelin & Kirilov
in Bull. Soc. Nat. Mosc. 14:374 (1841)

Aquilegia lactiflora ("milky flower") is endemic to central Asia in subalpine areas up to 3,000 meters (the type locality is in the Tarbagatai Mountains in what is now extreme eastern Kazakhstan). This is a glandular-pubescent species, rather similar to the North American *A. micrantha*, growing 40 to 80 cm high, with ternate or biternate basal leaves, the leaflets somewhat glabrous above and lightly downy beneath. The flowers are nodding or suberect, usually pubescent. The sepals are white (sometimes pink or very light purple), lanceolate to oblong, widely spreading, or even slightly reflexed, 15 to 20 mm long. The blades are oblong, or wedge-shaped, rounded at the tips, and may be white or yellow; the spurs, 15 to 25 mm long, are straight or slightly incurved at the tips, and are white, or pale purple if the sepals are so colored. The stamens are slightly exserted.

Aquilegia lactiflora is an uncommon species in cultivation, to say the least. Still, varietal names may linger here and there: *A. lactiflora* var.

microphylla, with smaller leaflets; var. *leucantha* with pure white flowers; var. *dichroantha*, with pale purple spurs and white or yellow blades. *Aquilegia darvasii*, or some spelling similar to this, is considered a synonym.

Aquilegia laramiensis A. Nelson
in First Rept. Fl. Wyo. 78 (1896)

Aquilegia laramiensis, endemic to the Laramie Mountains of south-central Wyoming (the type locality is Cottonwood Canyon at the base of Laramie Peak), is completely undeserving of Farrer's disparaging description of it as a "somewhat dim American of no special interest." The more generous Clay (1937) said that it "should not be casually dismissed,"

Aquilegia laramiensis. Drawing by Carolyn Crawford.

obviously reacting to Farrer's statement. It is similar to *A. saximontana* in having hooked, stout spurs, and grows to about the same height (20 cm or less), but has white flowers, sometimes tinged with green on the sepals, with stamens no longer than the blades. The basal leaves are glaucous and biternately compound, with leaflets not crowded together as they are in *A. saximontana.* Leaves and stems may be slightly hairy. The lanceolate sepals are greenish white, divergent, about 10 to 15 mm long; the spurs are white, hooked, 5 to 7 mm long. The blades are off-white, oblong, about 10 mm long. Once thought to be rare in the wild, *A. laramiensis* is more or less readily available in the trade. It is easily grown in a lightly shaded, well-watered scree and is, as Clay would no doubt have agreed, a first-rate columbine for the rock garden.

Aquilegia litardierei Briquet
in Prodr. Fl. Corse 1:589 (1910)

Aquilegia litardierei has not been seen since its discovery on Monte Incudine on Corsica in 1908. It was described as a small species, with weakly ascending stems to 12 cm, hairy near the inflorescence, with ternate basal leaves, the leaflets of which were reported to be more or less glabrous above and pilose beneath. Munz gives the species nodding blue-violet flowers, but *Flora d'Italia* says "fiori orrizontale," which direction is definitely not nodding. The sepals are spreading, acute or acuminate, 14 mm long, the blades are widely obovate, 12 mm long, and the divergent hooked spurs are about 8 mm long. The stamens were described as being slightly exserted.

I am not aware of any recent columbine expeditions to Corsica to find this species, but since the island is not a large one, *Aquilegia litardierei* may be safely presumed extinct. *Flora d'Italia* says nothing about its existence but shows a drawing of what must be a remarkable columbine, with a strangely flattened aspect seen sideways. Farrer, like many garden writers excited by the legendary and nonexistent, wrote of "the bright blue flower, large indeed for the plant, [with] a special beauty of its own."

Named after René de Litardière, French botanist and student of the Corsican flora.

Aquilegia longissima Gray ex S. Watson
in Proc. Amer. Acad. Arts & Sci. 17:317 (1882)

Aquilegia longissima (Plate 32) gets its name from the amazingly long, delicate spurs—sometimes over 150 mm long—attached to a slightly reduced version (in flower size) of *A. chrysantha. Aquilegia longissima* grows 50 to 120 cm high; distribution is from northern Mexico (the type locality is in Coahuila) into western Texas in the Chisos Mountains, along streams and in canyons, and in other places where moisture is constant. The basal leaves are triternate, the leaflets glabrous to pubescent on both sides. The lanceolate sepals are spreading, 25 to 30 mm long; the blades are spatulate or spatulate-obovate, widely spreading, 15 to 30 mm long. Munz gives a minimum spur length of 90 mm. The stamens are exserted.

As with the other yellow-flowered columbines, *Aquilegia longissima* has been proposed as a variety of *A. chrysantha*. It is distinct from that species most evidently in the almost absurdly long spurs, and the blades, which spread out almost horizontally. *Aquilegia longissima* has purportedly been used in producing a number of hybrids, but in most cases the spur lengths show these plants to be of *A. chrysantha* parentage instead.

The mysterious columbine from the Baboquivari Mountains in southern Arizona, described under *Aquilegia chrysantha*, is considered to be *A. longissima* in *Arizona Flora*, which also ascribes this species to plants growing in the Huachuca Mountains in Arizona (Kearney and Peebles 1951). This complicates matters even further; considering the wide separation between the Chisos Mountains and the Baboquivari and Huachuca Mountains (the whole width of New Mexico, and then some), it is more likely that these are variants of *A. chrysantha*, or, taking a more cosmic view of things, that *A. longissima* is only a variant of *A. chrysantha*.

Aquilegia micrantha Eastwood
in Proc. Calif. Acad. Sci. 4:559 (1895)

Aquilegia micrantha ("small-flowered"; Plates 34–36) is a widely variable species generally found growing on cliffs, in hanging gardens where they can get access to moisture seeping from above. *Aquilegia micrantha* is native to south-central Utah (the type locality is in southeastern Utah), northern Arizona, and southwestern Colorado. Height is 60 cm, or half that in sunnier, drier habitats. The basal leaves are bi- or triternately compound, the leaflets glabrous to pubescent above and viscid-pubescent beneath. The foliage is glandular-pubescent, the flowers are nodding or erect, glandular-pubescent. The sepals and spurs may be white, pink, or blue, which creates havoc for those trying to construct a key based on flower color. The sepals are oblanceolate, spreading, acuminate or obtuse, 10 to 20 mm long. The blades are more or less white, divergent or erect (that is, spreading away from the center of the flower in the direction of the blades), oblong, truncate, rounded at the edges, 5 to 10 mm long. The spurs are straight, or slightly spreading, slender, and 15 to 30 mm long. The stamens project about 5 mm beyond the end of the blades. A spurless form reported from southwestern Colorado, sometimes called *A. micrantha* var. *mancosana*, is presumably extinct but still listed in Colorado floras.

The Navajo and Kayenta used *Aquilegia micrantha* to aid childbirth (Moerman 1998).

Aquilegia moorcroftiana Wallich
in Catalog No. 4713 (1820)

Aquilegia moorcroftiana, found from Ladakh and Tibet westward into Afghanistan, grows at the highest elevation of any columbine, in the open or among low shrubs at elevations often exceeding 4,000 meters. The plants at this elevation may be only 20 cm high. At somewhat lower elevations the flowering stems reach 40 cm. The crowded basal leaves are biternate or mostly so, thick, and glaucous, glabrous above, slightly pubescent beneath. The stems themselves are pubescent and carry a few nodding flowers with spreading, blue-purple lanceolate-ovate sepals 13 to 18 mm long. The sepals are acute or somewhat obtuse (I am unable to bring myself to use Munz's word "obtusish" to describe anything at all). The blades are blue, rounded at the tips, occasionally with pale yellow margins, and 10 to 13 mm long. The spurs are blue-purple, slender, 12 to 17 mm long, and straight or slightly curved inward. The stamens are slightly exserted. Seed is sometimes available from rock garden society seed exchanges or from seed collectors traveling in the Himalayas.

A dwarf, more pubescent, more westerly distributed version of *Aquilegia moorcroftiana* is sometimes called *A. afghanica*, or *A. moorcroftiana* var. *afghanica*. This has stems 8 to 20 cm high, less nodding (the description is "subhorizontal") flowers of essentially the same color as *A. moorcroftiana* but with sepals 15 to 18 mm long, blades 10 to 12 mm long, straight spurs 15 to 17 mm long, and slightly exserted stamens. The type locality for this variety, or species, is the Kurram River Valley in Pakistan. Rechinger, calling it, as did Munz, *A. afghanica* in the *Flora Iranica*, suggested that this may be only a variant of what he considered to be the polymorphic *A. moorcroftiana*, but he had not seen specimens (nor, as I hope is obvious, have I) on which to base any firm decision.

Rather disconcertingly, the *Flora Iranica* also contains descriptions of four species of *Aquilegia* which, political situations being what they are, will in this country probably remain nothing but names for years to come. All but one have the notation "Species nova ex affinitate remota *Aquilegia moorcroftiana*," so I am including them here, hoping, somehow, that *A. moorcroftiana* is even more polymorphic than anyone suspects, and that these are just localized variants of this species. The *Flora Iranica* also provides the original citations, with the exception noted.

Aquilegia euchroma ("good color," or, possibly, referring to the staining of chromosomes, "genetically active"; originally described by Rechinger fils in Anz. Math.-Nat. Kl. Österr. Akad. Wiss. 91:77 in 1954) is endemic to Afghanistan. The type locality is in Badakshan Province in northeastern Afghanistan. It is described as reaching 40 to 60 cm in height, the stems more or less glabrous below, densely glandular-pubescent above, or throughout. The basal leaves are biternate, paler beneath, glabrous or more or less pubescent. The flowers are nodding, small, yellowish, drying (i.e., on herbarium sheets) purplish. The sepals are 8 to 11 mm long, the blades 6 mm long; the spurs are 11 to 16 mm long and purplish or purplish blue. The stamens are equal to the blades, or just slightly exserted.

Aquilegia gracillima ("very slender," possibly, although the Latin adjective can also mean "insignificant") is described as a densely cespitose plant with ternate basal leaves and glandular-pilose stems, the height of which is not given. The small white, rose-tinged flowers are nodding, the oblong or elliptic-lanceolate sepals 10 to 12 mm long, the blades 7 mm long, the slender spurs 15 to 17 mm long. This species was apparently described from a single specimen collected near Ghazni in eastern Afghanistan. *Aquilegia helmandica*, a species described in 1974, is considered a synonym.

Aquilegia maimanica, from Maimana (Meymaneh) Province in northwestern Afghanistan (the type locality is given as being near Belchiragh), is described as growing 40 to 60 cm tall with somewhat glabrous, simply branched stems with plentiful cauline leaves. The basal leaves are biternate; their leaflets are wedge-shaped. The suberect flowers are described as "pale blue and white"; the assumption is that the sepals and spurs are pale blue and the blades are white. The oblong-lanceolate sepals are about 20 mm long, and acuminate. The spurs are slender, lightly curved, and 20 to 25 mm long. The length of the blades, and of the stamens, curiously, is not given in the description, which is apparently based on two collections in the same region.

Aquilegia microcentra ("small center"), from Orozgan Province in southeastern Afghanistan, is described as being a densely cespitose plant with more or less glabrous, ternate basal leaves and stems (height not given) somewhat glabrous below and somewhat glandular and densely pubescent above. The inflorescence is densely pubescent. The small flowers are nodding, the slightly ovate-elliptic sepals are 10 mm long, acute, and white (at least in the dried specimen). The spurs are slightly longer than the sepals. This species was described from two specimens.

It is possible that these truly represent new species; more specimens need to be collected if botanists are to arrive at a definitive answer. Who would attempt to make the collections is another story altogether.

Aquilegia moorcroftiana, to return to the principal species, was named for William Moorcroft, explorer of Ladakh and Tibet, mountaineer, and author.

Aquilegia nigricans Baumgarten
in Enum. Stirp. Transsilv. 2:104 (1816)

Aquilegia nigricans ("becoming black") is quite similar to *A. atrata*, except that in *A. nigricans* the stems, which grow 30 to 60 cm high, are glandular-pubescent, and the dark purple flowers are larger. The sepals are spreading, ovate-lanceolate or elliptic, 25 to 35 mm long, the blades are oblong-obovate and 11 to 14 mm long, the spurs are strongly hooked, and about 15 mm long. The stamens are slightly exserted. Found in the mountains, usually on limestone, from Austria eastward into Hungary (the type locality is eastern Hungary), southward throughout the Balkans, and in at least one location in Greece (Strid 1986).

A dwarf plant reported from the Carpathian Mountains, *Aquilegia ullepitschii*, with stems to 20 cm and nodding dark flowers, with sepals 30 mm long, blades 30 mm long, and hooked spurs 15 mm long, may only be a localized form of *A. nigricans*.

A variety with sepals 18 to 20 mm long, only lightly glandular-pubescent in the uppermost part of the inflorescence, found in southern Austria, is sometimes called *Aquilegia nigricans* var. *ebneri* (to Munz, it was *A. vulgaris* var. *parviflora*). Some authorities recognize yet another variety of *A. nigricans*, var. *subscaposa*, from Romania. This has stems to 30 cm and bright blue flowers. Munz, surprisingly, considered this *A. nigricans* itself but did not acknowledge the less-black flower color.

Another species, *Aquilegia blecicii*, recently described from Montenegro (by Podobnik in Biosistematika 12:16 in 1986), is similar to *A. nigricans* but with larger, bicolored flowers, according to *Flora Europaea*. It may be another variety, if even that, of *A. nigricans*.

Aquilegia nivalis Falconer ex Jackson
in Ind. Kew. 1:167 (1893)

Aquilegia nivalis ("of snow") is a rare treasure. This is another high-altitude Himalayan columbine, found on alpine screes and slopes at 3,000 to 4,000 meters, from northern Pakistan to Himachal Pradesh in northwestern India (the type locality is in Kashmir). The plant is glandular-pubescent, with flowering stems that may reach 20 cm in gigantic specimens. The basal leaves are biternate, the leaflets glabrous above and mostly glabrous below. The flowers are relatively large, solitary on the stem, somewhat nodding or erect, with wide, large, oblong-ovate or ovate dark purple sepals. The sepals are 22 to 30 mm long, and divergent. The blades are small, truncate, about 10 mm long, hidden by the sepals when the flowers are nodding, and purple-black. The two-tone effect of this flower, with the darker blades, is quite striking. The spurs are very short, less than 10 mm long, curved inward at the tips or slightly saccate. The stamens are included, or almost so.

The occasional example of saccate spurs in *Aquilegia nivalis* has suggested to some that this is among the most primitive species of *Aquilegia*. Its habitat is also one of the highest in elevation of any species, exceeded only by *A. moorcroftiana*.

Farrer (1907) wrote, uncharacteristically laconically, that *Aquilegia nivalis* "is reported a small and special beauty"; a generation later, Clay (1937) called *A. nivalis* "a first-class plant." Little else has been written about this species, except to obfuscate the situation surrounding the name *A. vulgaris* subsp. *jucunda* that the *Flora of British India* unfortunately gave to this species in 1872, thus perpetuating a horrific confusion between *A. nivalis* and *A. glandulosa* (also stuck with the name *jucunda*) among writers for almost fifty years. Seed is very rarely available, and so we must be content with photographs and the terse comments of two of the greatest writers on plants of the high mountains.

Aquilegia olympica Boissier
in Ann. Sci. Nat. 14:360 (1841)

Aquilegia olympica (Plate 37) is a handsome species native to forests, meadows, and the subalpine regions in the Caucasus, the mountains of northern Turkey, and northern Iran. Munz gives Boissier's type locality as "Olympus Armenus"—that is, Keshish Dag in the Caucasus, not Greece. *Aquilegia olympica* (not to be confused with the 'Olympia' strain of hybrids) is a vulgaris-type, with densely glandular-pubescent stems and leaves (less so on the biternate basal leaves), with flowering stems to

60 cm. As in *A. vulgaris*, the leaflets are glabrous above and pilose beneath. The nodding flowers have long, spreading, ovate-acuminate sepals, 20 to 45 mm long, light purple, blue, or sometimes pink in color. The blades are the same color as the sepals and spurs, or white, 35 mm long, somewhat longer than those of typical *A. vulgaris*, relative to the sepal length. The spurs are stout, 10 to 20 mm long, strongly hooked, and the same color as the sepals. The length of the stamens is roughly equal to that of the blades.

The form with white blades has occasionally been called *Aquilegia olympica* var. *caucasica*. A horticultural form, *A. olympica* 'Flore Pleno', with doubled white blades, is also known. The species itself is doubtfully available in the trade, except in the form of wild-collected seed, available from Czech and other collectors.

Aquilegia olympica is nominally distinct from *A. vulgaris* in its wider sepals and longer blades, and its habitat, far distant from that of *A. vulgaris*. Even so, many botanists, in North America anyway, would probably subsume this species into the polymorphic *A. vulgaris*; in truth, plants of *A. olympica* I grew from seed collected in the Caucasus were very difficult to distinguish from *A. vulgaris*.

Munz, echoing the views of Bulavkina (1937), considered a species called *Aquilegia caucasica* to be synonymous with *A. olympica*. Imagine, then, my surprise in finding a Web site dedicated to endangered plants of Georgia in which *A. caucasica* is listed as a species in its own right, along with another species, *A. gegica*, for which I have found no information at all.

Aquilegia ottonis Orphanides
in Boissier, Diagn. Pl. Orient. Nov. 1:11 (1854)

Aquilegia ottonis, named for Otto, king of Greece from 1832 to 1862, is a variable complex found in damp, shady areas among calcareous rocks in the mountains of Greece, Albania, and Macedonia, with a disjunct population in south-central Italy. (The sudden presence of this species in central Italy and nowhere else on the peninsula might be the subject of much useless speculation, but see below.) The taxa involved have been considered species in their own right, as subspecies of other species now considered to be themselves subspecies of *A. ottonis*, and so on. The type itself, from Mount Chelmos in the Peloponnese in Greece, grows anywhere from 15 to 50 cm high, with usually glandular-pubescent leaves and stems. The basal leaves are ternate or biternate, the leaflets more or less glabrous above and hairy-glaucous beneath. The flowers are more or less nodding, the sepals blue-violet, oblong, roughly 18 mm long. The blades are white, or pale blue-violet, truncate at the ends, 15 mm long, or longer. The spurs are also pale blue-violet, about 14 mm long, and strongly hooked. The stamens are exserted.

Farrer thought this species was *Aquilegia olympica*, to which it is related (Strid 1986), but he did correctly describe *A. amaliae*, "a glandular Columbine from Thessaly, like a smaller *A. vulgaris*, with flowers of blue and white." Clay (1937) was silent on both *A. ottonis* and *A. amaliae*. I once grew *A. ottonis*, and have pleasant memories of it.

There are at least two subspecies of *Aquilegia ottonis*, both with blades shorter than 15 mm. Subspecies *amaliae* (*A. amaliae*, which used to be a species all by itself with its own solar system of subspecies; Amalia was queen of Greece, Otto's bride) is native to the montane and subalpine regions of the southern Balkans and Greece, on rock ledges in ravines, where the roots can find adequate moisture (Strid 1986). This subspecies, common on Mount Olympus, has branched flowering stems and rounded, white blades (in contrast to the truncate blades of the type), and glabrous leaves. The stamens are not exserted. Subspecies *taygetea* (*A. taygetea*), a rarity from montane and alpine zones (Strid says "damp calcareous screes in semi-shade") in Taygetos in southern Greece, has unbranched flowering stems, glandular-pubescent leaves and stems, glandular-pubescent flowers, and, again, stamens not exserted.

Munz reported another variety, *Aquilegia ottonis* var. *unguisepala*, described by the Hungarian botanist Borbás in 1882, with lanceolate-ovate sepals, from Mount Majella in central Italy. This variety is not recognized in either *Flora Europaea* or *Flora d'Italia*; the author of the treatment in *Flora d'Italia* notes the "doubtful identification" of the Italian plants and suggests they might be a new species or subspecies, but the description, and location, of var. *unguisepala* may partially solve the mystery of the Italian populations of *A. ottonis*.

Another species otherwise strongly resembling *Aquilegia ottonis*, *A. champagnatii*, was described from southern Italy in 1981. The leaves are said to be glabrous, and the spurs curved but not hooked. Munz said the spurs of both *A. ottonis* and (as he considered it) *A. amaliae* were curved (or, to be precise, "uncinate-curved") and not hooked, which is a lot of help.

Aquilegia oxysepala Trautvetter & C. F. Meyer
in Fl. Ochot. 10 (1856)

Aquilegia oxysepala ("acute sepals," "sharp sepals") started out as a species in its own right, eventually collecting a few varieties along the way, then was forced to spend some time under the aegis of *A. buergeriana* (as *A. buergeriana* var. *oxysepala*), shorn of its varieties, which simply disappeared. *Aquilegia oxysepala* is much more widely distributed than *A. buergeriana*, growing along streams in forested areas in Honshu, Hokkaido, Korea, eastern China, and Siberia. The type locality is given by Munz as "Udskoi, eastern Siberia." The basal leaves are biternate, glabrous above and glaucous beneath. The sepals are divergent, ovate-lanceolate, acuminate, purple, 20 to 30 mm long; the blades are pale yellow or yellowish white, oblong, 10 to 13 mm long. The spurs are purple, roughly 20 mm long and strongly hooked. This species, which differs from *A. buergeriana* in its strongly hooked spurs and barely exserted stamens, grows to 80 cm and is occasionally offered for sale.

The one variety besides the type, *Aquilegia oxysepala* var. *kansuensis*, is confined to central China and has sepals to 25 mm long; it is essentially a smaller version of *A. oxysepala* itself. A pale-flowered form, forma *pallidiflora*, has also been described.

The acuminate sepals and yellowish blades should be sufficient to distinguish *Aquilegia oxysepala* from *A. vulgaris*, to which it is otherwise rather alarmingly similar.

Chapter 8

Aquilegia pancicii Degen
in Magyar Bot. Lapok 4:118 (1905)

This species from Serbia (the type locality is the Suha Planina in Serbia) is described as growing to 50 cm, similar to *Aquilegia vulgaris* but with smaller flowers, triternate basal leaves, and densely glandular-pubescent leaves and stems. The flowers are nodding, blue; the sepals are oblanceolate, 20 mm long, the blades are truncate, 7 mm long, whitish at the tips. The spurs are curved inward; the staminodes are exserted.

Aquilegia pancicii is not in cultivation.

Named for the botanist Josef Pančić.

Aquilegia parviflora Ledebour
in Mém. Acad. Sci. Petersb. 5:544 (1815)

Aquilegia parviflora ("small-flowered"; Plate 38) is, as the name may indicate, a plant more for collectors than for gardeners who have to have every giant-flowered beauty and disdain those plants that choose to exist simply for their own sake. Yet Clay (1937) wrote that it "can be a desirable thing, with distant, thick-margined leaflets and bicoloured flowers, small, with unusually short spurs, but carried with grace and distinction."

Native to woodlands and slopes in eastern Siberia (the type locality is on the Lena River), northern China (Manchuria), northern Mongolia, and Sakhalin Island, *Aquilegia parviflora* grows to 40 cm, more or less, and has small biternate basal leaves, the leaflets glabrous above and glaucous below, with some soft hairs or covered with fine hairs. The glabrous stems are usually leafless. The long-pediceled flowers are suberect, or slightly nodding, with spreading blue-purple sepals, 15 to 20 mm long. The blades are blue-purple, or white, 3 to 5 mm long, the spurs short (less than 5 mm in length), strongly curved inward, and blue-purple. The stamens are exserted. Completely white forms may also be found.

Aquilegia pubescens Coville
in Contr. U.S. Natl. Herb. 4:56 (1893)

Aquilegia pubescens, named for its glandular-pubescent stems (not always present, naturally; the lower stems may be glabrous) is native to high elevations in the southern Sierra Nevada in California. The type locality is White Chief Mine in Tulare County, California. This is the only California species of *Aquilegia* with erect flowers. Plants grow to about 40 cm tall, with thick, ternate or biternate basal leaves and pink, yellow, or cream-colored sepals and spurs. The leaflets are glabrous or pubescent on both sides. The sepals are spreading, oblong, or lanceolate-ovate, more or less acute, 15 to 20 mm long. The oblong blades are 8 to 12 mm long. The spurs are straight, or spreading (outward) like those of *A. chrysantha* and *A. coerulea*. The flowers are glandular, with stamens exserted about 5 mm. The species is easily grown but not long-lived.

Like *Aquilegia micrantha*, *A. pubescens* causes trouble for those constructing keys to the genus arranged by flower color. Payson (1918) described its color as "canary yellow throughout"; he considered this species close to *A. chrysantha*, the principal differences being "the much less dissected leaves, lower habit of growth, and fewer, smaller flowers." In her wonderful book *Hardy Californians* (1936), Lester Rowntree wrote, "The immense flowers look upwards, pointing their long tails to earth, and run the entire color gamut of the long-spurred garden hybrids in every possible color combination—wine and yellow; yellow and white; pink, purple, blue, with cream or light yellow; cream or white flushed with various shades of red." It is likely that plants with flower colors other than yellow represent various degrees of introgression from *A. formosa*, which meets *A. pubescens* everywhere throughout the range of the latter (Grant 1952). In its habitat, *Aquilegia pubescens* occasionally comes into some degree of proximity to populations of *A. formosa*, a species of lower elevations. Some authors have suggested that the presence of pink spurs on plants of *A. pubescens* growing near the colonies of *A. formosa* are indicative of introgression from *A. formosa*, this despite the difference in pollinators.

Aquilegia pubiflora Wallich
in Catalog No. 4714 (1830)

Aquilegia pubiflora ("hairy flower"), a Himalayan species found at middle elevations (the type locality is in Srinagar), is fairly similar to *A. moorcroftiana* but grows at lower elevations (2,400 to 3,300 meters, according to Polunin and Stainton 1997). The plant, which is lightly hairy throughout, grows anywhere from 15 to 70 cm high. The basal leaves are biternate, glabrous above and lightly hairy on the undersides. The cauline leaves are linear and entire. The flowers are multiple (more than two per stem), nodding, puberulent, at least on the outside, blue-purple or darker red-purple in all parts. The oblanceolate sepals are spreading, long-acuminate, about 25 mm long. The blades are oblong-obovate and 10 to 15 mm long. The spurs are very short, 5 to 12 mm long and strongly hooked.

The plant, known to Clay (1937) as "a variable species of Western Himalaya, which may be blue or clarety, purple or bicoloured, or reputedly a more interesting yellow," is scarcely in cultivation, even in reputedly interesting colors.

Munz recognized one variety, which the *Flora of Himachal Pradesh* also recognizes, *Aquilegia pubiflora* var. *mussooriensis*, from the Mussooree Range in northern India. This has blue, purple, white, or even yellow flowers (interesting or not), with more or less acute sepals 15 mm long, blades 11 mm long, and spurs 4 to 7 mm long. Unfortunately for the sake of those who treasure taxonomic felicities, the name (now regarded as a synonym for the type) *A. pubiflora* var. *winterbottomiana* is no longer recognized.

Three other species that have affinities to *Aquilegia pubiflora*, all from Pakistan, have been described, each apparently from a single specimen. These are *A. kurramensis*, from the Kurram River area (south of the Khyber Pass) with obovate cauline leaves, the margins of which are incised, and lanceolate sepals; *A. chitralensis*, from Chitral in the Hindu Kush, with two pink flowers per stem, and 7-mm-long curved spurs; and *A. baluchistanica*, from Baluchistan, similar to *A. chitralensis* but with one to six flowers on the stem and spurs 15 to 25 mm long.

Plate 9. *Aquilegia alpina.* Photo by John Fielding.

Plate 10. *Aquilegia atrovinosa* in Kyrgyzstan. Photo by Dick Bartlett.

Plate 11. *Aquilegia bertolonii.* Photo by John Fielding.

Plate 12. *Aquilegia* 'Blue Berry' in the author's garden.

Plate 13. *Aquilegia brevistyla*,
Lawrence County, South Dakota.
Photo by Chuck Sheviak.

Plate 14. *Aquilegia* 'Bunting' in the
author's garden.

Plate 15. *Aquilegia canadensis*, Ottawa
Valley, Ontario. Photo by Ernie Boyd.

Plate 16. *Aquilegia chrysantha*. Photo by Charles Mann.

Plate 17. *Aquilegia chrysantha* 'Yellow Queen' in the author's garden.

Plate 18. *Aquilegia* 'Clematiflora', pink form, in John Drake's nursery. Photo by John Fielding.

Plate 19. *Aquilegia* 'Clematiflora Alba' in John Drake's nursery. Photo by John Fielding.

Plate 20. *Aquilegia coerulea*, Boreas Pass, Colorado.

Plate 21. *Aquilegia coerulea*, Ice Lake Trail, San Juan County, Colorado.
Photo by Charles Mann.

Plate 22. *Aquilegia coerulea* 'Crimson Star', Vail, Colorado.
Photo by Charles Mann.

Plate 23. *Aquilegia desertorum*.
Photo by Bill Jennings.

Plate 24. *Aquilegia elegantula*. Photo by Charles Mann.

Plate 25. *Aquilegia flabellata* 'Nana Alba'. Photo by Charles Mann.

Plate 26. *Aquilegia flabellata* 'Rosea'.

Plate 27. *Aquilegia flavescens*, Logan Pass, Waterton-Glacier International Peace Park. Photo by Ernie Boyd.

Plate 28. *Aquilegia formosa* var. *formosa*, near Eugene, Oregon.
Photo by Randy Tatroe.

Plate 29. *Aquilegia formosa* var. *truncata*. Photo by Charles Mann.

Plate 30. *Aquilegia glandulosa* in the author's garden.

Plate 32. *Aquilegia longissima.* Photo by John Fielding.

Plate 31. *Aquilegia jonesii* in the author's garden.

Plate 33. *Aquilegia* 'McKana's Giant' strain, red and yellow form.

Plate 34. *Aquilegia micrantha*, cream form, Grand County, Utah. Photo by Bill Jennings.

Plate 35. *Aquilegia micrantha*, yellow form, Montrose, Colorado. Photo by Bill Jennings.

Plate 40. *Aquilegia saximontana* in the author's garden.

Plate 41. *Aquilegia scopulorum*. Garden of Gwen Kelaidis.

Plate 42. *Aquilegia triternata* in the author's garden.

Plate 43. *Aquilegia vulgaris* 'Adelaide Addison'. Photo by Charles Mann.

Plate 44. *Aquilegia vulgaris* 'Double Pink' in John Drake's nursery. Photo by John Fielding.

Plate 46. *Aquilegia vulgaris* 'Greenapples'. Photo by John Fielding.

Plate 45. *Aquilegia vulgaris* 'Flore Pleno Burgundy' in John Drake's nursery. Photo by John Fielding.

Plate 49. *Aquilegia vulgaris* 'Stellata White'. Photo and planting design by John Fielding.

Plate 50. *Aquilegia vulgaris* 'Sweet Surprise'. Photo by John Fielding.

Plate 51. *Aquilegia vulgaris* 'Warwick' in John Drake's nursery. Photo by John Fielding.

Plate 52. *Aquilegia vulgaris* 'Woodside Purple'.
Photo and planting design by John Fielding.

Plate 53. *Paraquilegia anemonoides* in Kyrgyzstan. Photo by Dick Bartlett.

Aquilegia pyrenaica de Candolle
in Lamarck and de Candolle, Fl. Fr. 5:640 (1815)

Aquilegia pyrenaica, "a most important charmer which brings us on to debatable land strewn with the corpses of botanists dead in mutual war over its varieties and sub-species" (Farrer), represents another polymorphic complex into which species are subsumed and then separated out again. The species reaches 10 to 30 cm in height, with usually biternate basal leaves. The leaves and stems are almost glabrous or glandular-pubescent, becoming more pubescent in the inflorescence; the stems are often almost leafless. The flowers are nodding, blue, the ovate sepals spreading, to 3 cm long. The spurs are slender, straight or slightly incurved, 10 to 15 mm long. The blades are obovate, about 15 mm long, the stamens included, or of equal length to the blades, all forming, in Farrer's words, "the big and lovely dark-blue flower, invariably glorified by its central fluff of golden stamens."

Aquilegia pyrenaica itself is found, of course, in the Pyrenees and northeastern Spain (the type locality is given in Munz as "High Pyrenees"; the exact wording is "dans les rocailles et les prairies des Hautes Pyrénées"). *Flora Europaea* recognizes three subspecies (Munz, naturally, regarded these as distinct species, and recognized another, *A. aragonensis,* which is like *A. pyrenaica* but with smaller flowers, and which, should anyone care, was previously saddled with names like *A. discolor* var. *aragonensis* and *A. pyrenaica* var. *discolor* forma *aragonensis*), all of which have blades shorter (less than 9 mm) than the species; *Flora Iberica,* fortunately, considers *A. aragonensis* to be merely a synonym of *A. pyrenaica.*

Aquilegia pyrenaica subsp. *cazorlensis* (*A. cazorlensis*), from the Sierra de Cazorla and elsewhere in southeastern Spain, has ternate or biternate leaves, spurs slightly curved inward, and exserted stamens. The flowers are concolorous. The sepals are 11 to 16 mm long, and lanceolate. *Aquilegia pyrenaica* subsp. *discolor* (*A. discolor;* Plate 39; "a nice thing for the rather moister parts of the scree," Clay 1937) is a smaller plant, to 15 cm, from northwestern Spain, with more or less glabrous once-ternate basal leaves, ovate-lanceolate sepals 10 to 17 mm long, stamens not exserted, spurs slightly curved inward, and the blades sometimes white (hence the name *discolor*). *Aquilegia pyrenaica* subsp. *guarensis,* from the Sierra de

Guara in the central Pyrenees, is taller than subsp. *discolor*, and glandular-pubescent throughout. The sepals are lanceolate, 10 to 14 mm long, and, like subsp. *discolor*, the blades may be white. The stamens are not exserted.

Aquilegia pyrenaica is a fine species for the garden but susceptible to attack by aphids. *Aquilegia pyrenaica* subsp. *discolor* is occasionally available as seed or from mail-order nurseries (usually as plain old *A. discolor*) and is a first-rate plant for the rock garden (including moist screes), especially in its smaller forms, and even in these it will form cushions 40 cm wide under favorable conditions.

Aquilegia rockii Munz
in Gentes Herb. 7:95 (1946)

Aquilegia rockii (Plate 5) is found at elevations of about 3,500 meters in southwestern Sichuan, in the open and in forests, through northwestern Yunnan and adjacent areas of Tibet. The type locality is Mount Siga in Sichuan. The flowering stems, which have a distinct purple color, reach at least 60 cm. The basal leaves are biternate, the leaflets somewhat glabrous above and glaucous and softly downy beneath. The inflorescence is densely glandular-pubescent. The flowers are suberect or nodding, purplish red or blue, all of one color. The sepals are spreading, long-acuminate, 22 to 32 mm long. The blades are oblong, 12 to 16 mm long, the spurs are straight, 17 to 20 mm long, and slightly curved inward at the tips. The stamens are included.

Munz reported a collection of a plant similar to *Aquilegia rockii* but with spurs only 3 mm long, which he provisionally included with *A. ecalcarata*. He suggested that *A. rockii* was an intermediate between *A. ecalcarata* and *A. oxysepala* var. *kansuensis*; nevertheless, current treatments have upheld his name *A. rockii*, which he proposed in his monograph on *Aquilegia*. It shares the range of *A. oxysepala* var. *kansuensis* but occurs at higher elevations.

Named for the botanist and plant collector Joseph Rock.

Aquilegia saximontana Rydberg
in Gray, Syn. Fl. N. Amer. 1:43 (1895)

Aquilegia saximontana (Plate 40) is the third American species with hooked spurs. This subalpine and alpine species is quite similar to *A. laramiensis*, growing to 20 cm or less, except the leaflets in *A. saximontana* are usually more crowded together, and the foliage is completely glabrous. The basal leaves are biternate, the leaflets green above, slightly glaucous below. The flowers are nodding. The sepals are blue, 9 to 12 mm long, the blades are whitish yellowish, 7 to 8 mm long, the spurs are hooked, blue, and 3 to 7 mm long. The stamens are equal to the blades.

Aquilegia saximontana is, considering its popularity in cultivation (only a recent popularity—of this species, Farrer sighed, "[It is] only a hope and nothing more"), a rare inhabitant of the Rocky Mountains (whence its specific epithet), found at high elevations in north-central Colorado, growing among rocks. In its habitat it is one of the least obvious of plants, barely noticeable when out of flower, and only a little more so when in flower. *Aquilegia saximontana* is not very floriferous in the wild; a colony, which may contain only a dozen plants, may have a total of four flowers, if that.

In cultivation, *Aquilegia saximontana* is much more floriferous and easily grown in a shaded scree. A reputed cross of this with the much less tractable *A. jonesii* is offered in the trade, but all plants I have seen so labeled were *A. flabellata* var. *pumila*.

Aquilegia scopulorum Tidestrom
in Amer. Midland Naturalist 1:167 (1910)

Aquilegia scopulorum ("of rocks"; Plate 41) is, in effect, a dwarf version of *A. coerulea*, forming a cushion of densely crowded biternately compound, glaucous basal leaves (similar to those of *A. jonesii*) but with relatively enormous (about 50 mm long) erect flowers. Clay (1937) offers a better description: "a dwarf and lovely high-alpine, to be pictured as a tiny tuft of leaves, each leaf a huddled mass of tiny overlapping leaflets, generally described as more or less downy, but in the form best known here almost bare and somewhat blue." The stems, as Clay suggested, as glabrous below and viscid-pubescent above, or throughout. The leaflets are glabrous. The sepals, spurs and blades are variously blue, pale blue, white. The sepals are spreading, oblong, 15 to 20 mm long, obtuse or somewhat pointed at the tips. The blades are white, blue, or sometimes white tinged with yellow, oblong, 10 to 12 mm long; the spurs are straight, 25 to 35 mm long. The stamens are slightly included, or exserted a few millimeters. The plant is about 10 cm tall in flower and forms cushions about as wide. Distribution of this ravishing plant is from central Utah (the type locality is Wasatch Peak in Utah) to central and southern Nevada, on limestone at high elevations.

The similarity of the flower of *Aquilegia scopulorum* to that of *A. coerulea* has caused some botanists to recommend resurrection of the old name, *A. coerulea* var. *calcarea.* Dwarf populations of *A. coerulea* from high elevations, even in Colorado, to the far east of the range of *A. scopulorum,* do not look all that much different from *A. scopulorum.* Populations of *A. scopulorum* in the Tushar Mountains in Utah have the green leaves of *A. coerulea,* which strongly suggests that *A. scopulorum* really is but a dwarf version of *A. coerulea* (Welsh et al. 1987). *Aquilegia scopulorum* has reportedly been found just recently in extreme southwestern Colorado, but I have not seen the specimens.

Munz, rather oddly, believed that the name *Aquilegia coerulea* var. *calcarea* referred to a variety with glandular-pubescent petioles. The form with red-tinged sepals and blades, from the Charleston Mountains in southern Nevada, was at one time called *A. scopulorum* var. *perplexans;* this name is still seen occasionally in seed lists.

Cultivation requirements for *Aquilegia scopulorum* are similar to those of other subalpine and alpine species: a deep scree, full sun or partial shade, plenty of moisture in spring, and nutrients provided in late winter ("for the choice and not too hotly arid scree," Clay 1937). In its time, in full flower, this is possibly the most beautiful plant in the rock garden. *Aquilegia scopulorum* seems to be short-lived in the garden, although the finger of blame for the repeated early demise of the many plants that have passed under my care could, just possibly, be pointed directly at me.

Aquilegia shockleyi Eastwood
in Bull. Torr. Bot. Club 32:193 (1905)

Aquilegia shockleyi, a species similar to *A. formosa* but with triternately compound and pale green glabrous basal leaves, grows around springs and other wet areas in Nevada (the type locality is Soda Springs Canyon) and across the California border into the Mojave Desert. This species grows 40 to 80 cm high. The leaflets are green and glabrous above and more or less glaucous beneath, and somewhat viscid. The flowers are nodding, glandular-pubescent, the sepals are red, spreading, occasionally with tinges of yellow or green, 10 to 20 mm long, lanceolate, or sometimes elliptic. The red, pink, or yellow-red spurs are 12 to 25 mm long and have the characteristic shape of many of the red-flowered columbines: stout near the flower, then narrow, then bulging at the tip. The blades are yellow, 3 to 5 mm long. The stamens are exserted.

In his 1918 monograph, Payson described two subspecies of *Aquilegia formosa*: *A. formosa* subsp. *dissecta*, with triternate leaves and thick spurs, and *A. formosa* subsp. *caelifax*, with triternate leaves and slender spurs. Specimens of both had been collected in the range of what Munz later considered to be a wider range for *A. shockleyi* than Payson had documented; Payson believed the populations at Soda Springs were the only ones that should be given the name *A. shockleyi*. Given the considerable variation of *A. formosa* it is perhaps understandable that some botanists now believe *A. shockleyi* to be only a regional variant of *A. formosa*; Eastwood's name is not upheld in the new *Jepson Manual*.

Plants true to name are available in the trade. They linger briefly in the garden, set seed, sow it where they may, and then hurriedly depart this earth.

Named for William H. Shockley, a mining engineer who collected specimens in western Nevada and adjacent areas of California in the late nineteenth century.

Aquilegia sibirica Lambert
in Encyc. 1:150 (1783)

Aquilegia sibirica is a fine species from, naturally, Siberia, and also northern Mongolia, generally growing in open areas. The leafless flowering stems may reach 60 cm or more. The upper parts of the stems and the petioles are sparsely hairy, according to *Flora of the U.S.S.R.*, which contradicts Munz's (and everyone else's) statement that the petioles are glabrous. The half-dozen or so specimens cited by Munz were possibly not representative, or the sparse hairs are so sparse as to make the adjective "glabrous" almost appropriate, or perhaps the hairs on this species do not travel well. Plants of *A. sibirica* in my garden, grown from seed collected in the Altai Mountains, have petioles that are glabrous, or so nearly so as to make little difference.

The basal leaves are usually ternate, sometimes biternate, and not plentiful. The leaflets are glaucous and glabrous. The flowers are nodding, borne severally on the stems, the sepals blue or wine-purple (or almost white), spreading and obtuse, about 30 mm long, sometimes slightly recurved at the tips. The blades are blue or white, about 12 mm long; the spurs are blue, 5 to 15 mm long, stout and strongly hooked. The stamens are equal to the length of the blades or slightly exserted. Plants with white blades are sometimes called *A. sibirica* var. *discolor*; plants with blue blades are sometimes called var. *concolor*.

According to Munz there was at one time a cross of *Aquilegia sibirica* and *A. vulgaris* made by "Miss Garnier of Wickham, England," and called *A. ×garnieriana*; there are also some doubles offered under the name *A. bicolor* which may or may not have had some *A. sibirica* genes in them. No doubt the bicolor name surfaces from time to time in any case; it is a name likely to be encountered even with entirely different parents.

Wild-collected seed of *Aquilegia sibirica* used to be available from the private seed lists of Czech collectors, but unfortunately this source is now effectively closed to American gardeners. This is a truly wonderful plant for the rock garden (probably much less effective in a perennial border); its low cluster of basal leaves hardly prepares the expectant gardener for the large, beautiful vulgaris-type flowers dancing atop the almost invisible stems.

The Species

Aquilegia skinneri Hooker
in Bot. Mag. t. 3919 (1842)

Aquilegia skinneri is an exclusively Mexican species, found mostly in Durango and Chihuahua (the type locality is given, absurdly, as "Guatemala") growing 60 to 100 cm high, with triternately compound, glabrous basal leaves. The leaflets are glabrous above and glaucous-pilose beneath. The slightly puberulent flowers are large, nodding, the sepals are lanceolate, yellow-green, 18 to 28 mm long, acuminate, and erect (like those of *A. canadensis*), or more or less spreading. The blades are green, or sort of green, 8 to 10 mm long and truncate, rounded at the edges; the spurs are pale red, straight, 35 to 50 mm long, stout at the base but abruptly narrowed in the middle and quite slender at the tips. The stamens are exserted.

Even with its spurs being at least a shade of red, Payson (1918) suggested that *Aquilegia skinneri* was pollinated by moths instead of hummingbirds. At one time it was believed that the type species represented a more southerly distributed plant, the type locality of Guatemala presumably having been taken seriously, and the plants of northern Mexico, supposedly being larger in all or most of their parts, were called *A. madrensis*.

There used to be a horticultural variety with doubled blades, *Aquilegia skinneri* var. *flore-pleno*, which has long since vanished from the trade. Munz stated that the species was common in horticulture, but that was over fifty years ago. Every plant I have seen labeled *A. skinneri* was *A. formosa* or something not even remotely like either one. Wild-collected seed is occasionally offered by Southwestern Native Seeds.

'Tequila Sunrise', a beautiful sunset-orange cultivar, is associated in the trade with *Aquilegia skinneri*, for reasons unknown to me. It has the characteristic shape, in every respect, of *A. formosa* var. *formosa*. It also lives with ease through a Colorado winter, which the true *A. skinneri*, from seed collected in the wild, has never done.

Aquilegia skinneri was named for the botanist George Ure Skinner.

Aquilegia thalictrifolia Schott & Kotschy
in Verh. Bot. Zool. Ver. Wien 3:130 (1853)

Aquilegia thalictrifolia, the columbine with leaves like *Thalictrum* (meadow rue), is an uncommon species found in northern Italy (the type locality is Storo in the Tyrol), on limestone rocks in damp shade. Leaflets aside, it is similar to, but somewhat larger than, *A. einseleana*, except that it is glandular-pubescent throughout. The basal leaves are biternate, the leaflets 10 to 30 mm long, and widely separated, looking nothing like any other columbine, or any meadow rue, for that matter. The blue-violet flowers are nodding or suberect, held on stems to 60 cm high. The sepals are spreading, about 20 mm long; the spurs are straight, or very slightly curved, and about 10 cm long. The blades are wedge-shaped, rounded at the ends. The stamens are just slightly exserted.

Aquilegia thalictrifolia has, in the past, been associated taxonomically with *A. einseleana*. The two species share the same range, although *A. thalictrifolia* grows at somewhat lower elevations; the two species are said to intergrade, and a form, *A. thalictrifolia* forma *intermedia*, may represent the results of these chance meetings.

This species is rarely offered in the trade, although seed is occasionally available from rock garden societies. Not to be confused with *Thalictrum aquilegiifolium* (who ever said taxonomists have no sense of humor?).

Aquilegia transsilvanica Schur
in Verh. Mitt. Siebenb. Ver. Naturw. 4:31 (1853)

Aquilegia transsilvanica comes from somewhere in the Carpathian Mountains. There seems to be some disagreement in the treatments as to where exactly in the Carpathians this species actually grows; Munz says Siebenbürgen in "eastern Hungary," *Flora Europaea* says Romania and Russia, but the *Flora of the U.S.S.R.* does not acknowledge its existence. It is a suitably mysterious situation.

The species grows to 45 cm, with biternate basal leaves, the leaflets glabrous above and slightly hairy beneath. The stems are more or less hairless below, but downy toward the inflorescence, with few if any stem leaves. The flowers are blue-violet, and nodding. The sepals are spreading, elliptic-ovate, 30 to 40 mm long and 16 to 25 mm wide; the blades are elliptic-ovate, about 25 mm long, rounded at the ends. The spurs are 10 mm long, and either "strongly hooked" (*Flora Europaea*) or "curved but not hooked" (Munz). The stamens are included.

I have not—obviously—seen this species. Munz based his description on Schur's original description and the one specimen he had seen (which is perfectly acceptable). He noted the curious similarity between *Aquilegia transsilvanica* and *A. glandulosa*, which grows a third of the way again across Asia: "The leaves seem less pubescent, the spurs less hooked and more slender at the base, sepals rounded at the apex." Huge geographical distances between the two species' habitats notwithstanding, are these minute differences sufficient to call them two distinct species? Clay (1937), thinking years ahead of me, called *A. transsilvanica* "a splendid plant which, I fancy, will prove to be identical with, or perhaps an even neater-foliaged form of, the *A. glandulosa* we already know."

Aquilegia triternata Payson
in Contr. U.S. Natl. Herb. 20:147 (1918)

Aquilegia triternata (Plate 42), the barrel columbine (who knows whence the common name?), is found at high elevations in eastern and south-eastern Arizona "in the mountains in Apache, Cochise, Santa Cruz, and Pima counties" (Kearney and Peebles 1951); the type locality is in the Chiricahua Mountains and adjacent western New Mexico. *Aquilegia triternata* grows to 60 cm, has green, usually triternate basal leaves, the leaflets glabrous or pilose above and glabrous or pilose beneath. The flowers are nodding, the sepals are ovate-lanceolate, red, slightly spreading, more or less acuminate, 12 to 20 mm long. The spurs are light red, stout, then narrowing abruptly about halfway to the tips, straight, and about 25 mm long. The blades are yellow, or yellow tinged with red, 7 or 8 mm long, and bluntly rounded at the tips. The stamens are exserted about 10 mm past the tips of the blades.

Aquilegia triternata, despite some claims to the contrary, is not found in western Colorado; the source of this confusion is discussed under *A.*

barnebyi. Plants identified as *A. formosa* in the Sandia Mountains of New Mexico are referable to *A. triternata*.

Flora of North America has subsumed this species into the similar *Aquilegia desertorum*, stating that the basal leaves are not reliably triternate. Most other treatments acknowledge the tendency of *A. triternata* to have occasionally biternate leaves; *A. triternata* has longer sepals and blades, and *A. desertorum* is confined to northern Arizona. Payson (1918) wrote that "the extreme differentiation of *A. triternata* occurs in southern Arizona," and that the species' "copious pubescence [is] well-marked and quite constant in appearance in the specimens from southern Arizona, but is often almost entirely lacking in plants from New Mexico." Wild-collected seed is readily available for gardeners to compare the two taxa, and *A. canadensis* as well. It is a beautiful plant of easy culture, and not troubled by aphids.

Aquilegia triternata has been used to treat headaches in ceremonies by the Navajo and Kayenta (Moerman 1998).

Aquilegia turczaninovii Kamelin & Gubanov
in Byull. Mosk. Obshch. Ispt. Prir. Biol. 96(6):114 (1991)

Synonyms: *Aquilegia leptoceras* Fischer & Meyer, in Ind. Sem. Hort. Petrop. 4:33 (1837); *A. brachyceras* Fischer & Meyer ex Turczaninov.

Aquilegia turczaninovii is a native of forests in eastern Siberia (*Flora of the U.S.S.R.*, using the name *A. leptoceras*, says "described from Transbaikalia," which must be somewhere east of Lake Baikal), about 20 to 30 cm tall in flower, with ternate or biternate basal leaves, the leaflets glabrous on both sides. The flowers are nodding, the oblong-ovate sepals are spreading, blue-purple, about 20 mm long, sometimes tipped with green; the ovate blades are blue or blue-purple, rounded or truncate, 10 to 12 mm long, sometimes with an off-white margin. The spurs are fairly stout and curved inward, about 15 mm long. The stamens are exserted about 5 mm.

Munz preferred to call this species *Aquilegia brachyceras* since Nuttall had used the now-discarded name *A. leptocera* (for *A. coerulea* var. *ochroleuca*) a few years before this species was described as *A. leptoceras*. *Flora of the U.S.S.R.* considered the name *brachyceras* a *nomen nudum* ("naked name," a name without an accompanying description, which invalidates it according to the accepted rules of modern nomenclature). The new name, *A. turczaninovii*, while being slightly less easy on the tongue, effectively deals with the nomenclatural problems and dispenses with the two names that seem better attached to dinosaurs. In any case, this species is so far on the fringe of columbine consciousness, let alone cultivation, that it hardly seems to make any difference at all what name is used.

Named, currently anyway, for the Russian botanist Nikolai Turczaninov.

Aquilegia viridiflora Pallas
in Nova Act. Acad. Petrop. 260, t. 11 (1779)

Aquilegia viridiflora ("green flower") is, obviously, a green-flowered columbine, although not exactly so. It is certainly one of the strangest species, although strange in a good sense. This is a finely pubescent plant with flowering stems reaching 45 cm; the basal leaves are biternate, the thick leaflets more or less glabrous above and downy beneath. The flowers are nodding, or slightly suberect. The sepals are green, oblong, 11 to 14 mm long, and barely spreading. The blades themselves are reddish brown, purplish, or yellowish green, wedge-shaped, as wide as they are long. The spurs are similarly colored, straight, or slightly incurved at the tips, and about 15 mm long. The stamens are exserted, usually.

Aquilegia viridiflora is native to rocky areas from the Altai Mountains eastward through northern China to the Amur River. The variety *atropurpurea* (sometimes considered a separate species; Plate 6) is the form with purplish blades and is available commercially, usually as seed. The seed is sometimes billed as 'Chocolate Soldier', as though this were a cultivar name rather than a descriptive made-up common name.

A lot of inconsiderate sentences have been written deriding the appearance and garden value of *Aquilegia viridiflora*, although Farrer described it as "an unshowy but pretty little blackish-flowered fragrant species from N. Asia, which has never made good its hold in English gardens, though it is often being introduced, and cherished as a rarity." Certainly, compared to some of the less inhibited species and hybrids, this plant has less impact in the garden, but even so, I think it is a fairly wonderful plant, and very much worth growing. A reasonable life span might be three years.

Aquilegia viscosa Gouan
in Fl. Monsp. 267 (1765)

Aquilegia viscosa ("sticky") is a vulgaris-like species found from southern France to northeastern Spain (and elsewhere, as we shall see), growing to 100 cm or so, with glandular-hairy leaves and viscid stems. The basal leaves are usually biternate, sometimes once-ternate, the leaflets sessile, pubescent above and glandular-hairy beneath. The flowers are nodding, usually blue or lilac-blue, occasionally white. The sepals are spreading, lanceolate-ovate, about 25 mm long; the oblong blades are 12 mm long, the spurs are 15 to 20 mm long, pubescent, and strongly hooked. The stamens are exserted.

Flora Europaea recognizes a subspecies, *Aquilegia viscosa* subsp. *hirsutissima* (which the authors indicate is synonymous with *A. montsicciana*, considered a distinct species by Munz). This is a shorter plant, 15 to 35 cm tall, with stamens included, or equal to the blades. While the type is supposedly restricted to southern France, subsp. *hirsutissima* is also found there and westward to the Pyrenees in northeastern Spain.

For some unknown reason, *Flora d'Italia* lists, and correctly describes, *Aquilegia viscosa*; the maps show it distributed from central Italy southward, in oak and beech woodland, but not in Sicily. Why no other treatment mentions southern Italy is yet another of the unnerving puzzles surrounding this genus.

Aquilegia vulgaris Linnaeus
in Sp. Pl. 533 (1753)

Aquilegia vulgaris ("common"; Plate 7) is the genotype and the most widely distributed and variable species in the genus. *Aquilegia vulgaris* is found from southern Scandinavia throughout Europe, in every country of western, central, and southern Europe, and in Morocco. It has also naturalized in North America.

Whether a species is native or naturalized is not always so easy to determine. Some texts suggest that the plant has moved eastward into Russia through naturalization; this would only be an acceptable interpretation if it could be demonstrated that the plants did not at one time grow there. Species increase their range through exactly the same process as naturalization; identifying some plant populations as naturalized and some as native assumes that the expansion of habitat stops the minute a species is described by a botanist, and relies too much on the artificiality of national boundaries, which plants do not respect. Obviously the populations of *Aquilegia vulgaris* in North America are naturalized, but arguments that European populations are naturalized without prior evidence of the species not existing there are tenuous at best.

The basic plant grows anywhere from 30 to 90 cm or more, with subglabrous or lightly hairy stems below, and becoming more hairy, sometimes glandular-hairy above, in the inflorescence. The basal leaves are biternate, the leaflets glabrous above and pilose beneath. The flowers are nodding, usually bluish violet, sometimes rose-colored or white; the sepals are spreading, lanceolate-ovate, 18 to 25 mm long, the spurs are 15 to 25 mm long and strongly hooked, very occasionally curved, but not straight. The blades are oblong-obovate and about 12 mm long. The stamens are equal in length to the blades, or sometimes slightly exserted about 2 mm.

Flora Europaea recognizes three subspecies besides the type, all from Spain; Spanish botanists seem to have taken seriously the polymorphic nature of *Aquilegia vulgaris*. Subsp. *dichroa* (*A. dichroa*; "two-colored"), from western Spain and Portugal, has the tips of the sepals tinged with white, and blades with white tips. The sepals are usually shorter than 20 mm. The stems are glandular-pubescent.

Aquilegia vulgaris subsp. *nevadensis* (*A. nevadensis*), from the Sierra Nevada in southern Spain, has densely glandular-pubescent herbage and slightly curved, not hooked, spurs. The sepals are blue, 15 to 25 mm long; the spurs and blades are also blue. The blades are roughly as long as the spurs. Subsp. *paui* (*A. paui*), from northeastern Spain (Catalonia), has herbage like typical *A. vulgaris* but with usually once-ternate basal leaves. Like subsp. *dichroa*, the sepals are tipped with white; the blades may be bluish violet or white. The blades are usually quite conspicuously longer than the spurs.

Aquilegia nuragica, a recently described (1978) species from Sardinia, is said to be similar to *A. vulgaris* but has much less glandular leaves and stems, and more or less suberect flowers.

There remain the two dozen other varieties of *Aquilegia vulgaris* recognized, or at least mentioned, by Munz in his monograph. (Munz considered the three Spanish and Portuguese varieties to be distinct species.) These varieties represent murky water indeed and cannot be navigated, let alone dived into, without several years' worth of provisions. Briefly (well, relatively briefly), these are var. *aggericola*, leaflets deeply incised, from southern France; var. *arbascensis*, sepals 30 mm long on a pubescent plant, from Haute-Garonne in France; var. *collina*, leaves not glandular-pilose and follicle rounded at the base, with sepals longer than the blades and spurs taken together, from the Valais in Swizerland and Jura in France; var. *cyclophylla*, with truncate blades and saccate spurs, from southwestern France; var. *dumeticola*, leaves not glandular-pilose but stems glandular-pubescent, from Corsica (curiously, *Flora d'Italia* does not mention the presence of *A. vulgaris* in Corsica—could *A. vulgaris* var. *dumeticola* be *A. nuragica*?).

Aquilegia vulgaris var. *eynensis* is similar to var. *aggericola*, but the leaflets are shallowly incised, from the Pyrenees; var. *glabella* is entirely glabrous, from Hungary; var. *glandulosa-pilosa* is, you guessed it, entirely glandular-pilose, from Montenegro (Crna Gora) and Bosnia and Hercegovina; var. *hispanica* has tubular spurs and pubescent leaves, from Spain (*Flora Iberica* at least provisionally upholds this variety); var. *incisa* from Bosnia and Hercegovina has triternate leaves; var. *longisepala*, from Hungary, has glabrous leaves and (I know this is hard to believe) extremely long sepals; var. *mollis*, from the southwest of France and the Pyrenees, is softly downy-hairy; var. *nemoralis*, from western Switzerland and France, has narrowly ovate sepals less than 18 mm long, spurs 14 mm long.

Aquilegia vulgaris var. *nivea* is all white. Munz gives its locations as "mostly in gardens, seldom wild (Germany, Hungary)." *Aquilegia vulgaris* var. *notabilis*, from Bosnia, Croatia, and Slovenia (probably) and southern Austria (maybe—when an Austrian botanist writing in the last part of the nineteenth century says "lower Austria," they usually mean Croatia and Slovenia), has ternate leaves; var. *parviflora*, which actually *is* from lower Austria, has sepals slightly longer than those of var. *nemoralis* and spurs slightly shorter, with red-blue flowers; var. *praecox*, from France, like var. *collina* but with shorter sepals; var. *ruscinonensis*, from the eastern Pyrenees, leaves pubescent only on the undersides, and spurs longer than the blades; var. *salvatoriana* (not mentioned by Munz), more like *A. bertolonii* but with hooked spurs; var. *sicula*, with stems glandular-pubescent above and obovate leaflets, from Sicily; var. *subalpina*, with sepals greater than 30 mm long, from southeastern France westward into true lower Austria, southward to Bosnia; and var. *subtomentosa*, from the Czech Republic, the stems densely hairy, the leaves softly hairy beneath, almost tomentose (densely hairy). There are even more names.

And yet . . . botanists remain the sanest of people. Two more varieties are of greater interest. One is *Aquilegia vulgaris* var. *ballii*, from the Atlas Mountains of Morocco, with bi- to triternate basal leaves, glabrous above, white, green-tipped sepals 15 to 25 mm long, white truncate blades, and blue, curved spurs. This is the only *Aquilegia* species found in Africa.

The other variety, *Aquilegia vulgaris* var. *stellata*, is less interesting as a botanical entity than it is for horticulture. The so-called stellate forms of *A. vulgaris*, which used to travel under this varietal name, are spurless. But current botanical treatments do not recognize spurless forms of any *Aquilegia* species at the varietal level; it is therefore probably best to label these "stellate" types, which offer nodding flowers in a range of colors, as 'Stellata' plus the color form—*A. vulgaris* 'Stellata White' (Plate 49), for example. *Aquilegia vulgaris* 'Greenapples' (or 'Green Apples'; Plate 46) is a pale green-flowered form.

The horticultural name *Aquilegia* ×*clematiflora* is sometimes given to the "stellate" forms of *A. vulgaris*, but there is apparently no basis for this. More often the name is used to identify spurless forms of hybrids involving *A. coerulea*, which are said to have larger flowers than those included under *A. vulgaris* var. *stellata*. Some sources suggest that *A.* ×*clematiquila* was the name originally used for these spurless plants; in any case, neither *A.* ×*clematiflora* nor *A.* ×*clematiquila* has any taxonomic validity.

A few other names associated with *Aquilegia vulgaris* pop up now and then in the trade. One is *A. baikalensis* (*A. baicalensis*), said to be a dwarf version of *A. vulgaris* but doubtfully coming from Lake Baikal; my seed never germinated after I tipped the pot over in a moment of carelessness.

Other selections of *Aquilegia vulgaris* are equally beautiful: the violet and white 'Adelaide Addison' (Plate 43) with doubled blades; the rose-colored 'Michael Stromminger'; the gorgeous dark purple, almost black, 'William Guiness' (Plate 8), also offered as 'Magpie'. 'Munstead White' (Plate 47) is a ravishing pure white, named after a selection favored by Gertrude Jekyll.

'Plum Pudding' is said to be a plum-violet double with short spurs, growing to 90 cm. 'Double Pink' (Plate 44) has, as might be guessed, doubled pink flowers. 'Melton Rapids' is a double with blue flowers; 'Raspberry Tart' is a double with red flowers, about 45 cm high. 'Winkie Red' is a dwarf selection, not doubled, with red flowers. 'Sweet Surprise' (Plate 50), a beautiful pale yellow, is possibly a hybrid.

A selection of *Aquilegia vulgaris* with variegated leaves, said to be a shy-flowering plant, is sometimes called 'Woodside Purple' (or 'Variegata' or 'Woodside Variegated' or *A. vervaneaea*; Plate 52). These names may represent slightly different cultivars. In relentlessly sunny climates such as mine, variegated leaves often have a diseased look about them; in cloudier climates they can be quite attractive, as the photograph demonstrates.

Aquilegia vulgaris is a truly protean species whose true nature may be less aptly delineated by pressed specimens in herbaria than by the multitude of horticultural forms that have persisted for centuries. The tendency of columbines, and of *A. vulgaris* in particular, to produce spurless flowers, or to explode in a frenzy of doubled or tripled petals, has resulted in a profusion of cultivars, some with a quite fantastic look to them, some more like the flowers of hops than of columbines. Growing them gives one a pleasant sense of continuity with gardeners down through the ages, although some of the odder forms are more than difficult to find in the trade in this country.

Whether or not these plants ultimately come from pure *Aquilegia vulgaris* is difficult to say. Parkinson and other gardeners of his time were fully aware of species outside of England, and no doubt some of these were grown in English gardens. One can see, however, from the plethora of varieties named by Munz that *A. vulgaris* is constantly redefining its image in its own manner, wherever it appears in the wild; and of course, in gardens the observation and care of plants is that much more acute. Parkinson wrote that his "Aquilegia inversis corniculis," a bizarre form with doubled upside-down flowers (not upward-facing: the flower faces downward but the parts are all upside-down), came true from seed. But these genuine oddities may have fallen out of favor with the gardening public and have recently been lamented as being apparently lost to cultivation.

Parkinson seemed to have fancied forms with doubled blades; he wrote, in *Paradisi in Sole Paradisus Terrestris* (1629), that "both single and double [are] carefully noursed up in our Gardens, for the delight both of their forme and colours." The cultivar sometimes called 'Double Pleat', violet and white, looks something more like a columbine from Mars than one from Earth, but with an old-fashioned-petticoat look that is utterly charming and is perhaps as close as we can come to Parkinson's vision of the full potential of the "colombine." 'Warwick', a cultivar with multiple petals, seems determined to look as little like an aquilegia as possible, yet it is a lovely flower in its own way, as Plate 51 shows. 'Burgundy', or, to be precise, *A. vulgaris* 'Flore Pleno Burgundy' (Plate 45), is another of these selections, photographed at the nursery of John Drake, custodian of the National Collection of Aquilegias in the United Kingdom.

Other cultivars with doubled or even tripled flowers are 'Trevor Bath', whose semi-double white flowers have short, pale red spurs; the Spring Song series of mixed colors and sometimes doubled flowers; and the rather peculiar 'Mrs. Nicholls', triple blue and white but without, unfortunately, fifteen spurs to complete the presentation.

'Nora Barlow' (Plate 48) is a mutant spurless form of *Aquilegia vulgaris* with multiple, short, rose and green petals, somewhat reminiscent of an astrantia, not at all reminiscent of a columbine ("an ugly flower but different," Lloyd 2000). Or, it looks somewhat like a columbine that stuck its finger into an electrical outlet by mistake. Perhaps inconsiderately named for a relative of Darwin's, 'Nora Barlow' has been propagated for more than two hundred years. 'Black Barlow' is a very dark purple variation, with the same slightly frazzled appearance; 'Ruby Port' is a dark-red version. The "Barlow look" is popular with seed companies, and different strains with the name Barlow in them have appeared. All promise to be spurless, with the almost emaciated, multiple sepals characteristic of the original 'Nora Barlow'.

Some firms, notably Plantworld® in the United Kingdom, continue work breeding forms of *Aquilegia vulgaris*—singles, doubles, triples, different patterns of leaf variegation, and so on. Perhaps the best way to view the possible number of variations within *A. vulgaris* is as an open-ended set whose beginning is expressed by the simplest example of pure *A. vulgaris*, and whose end stretches outward to infinity.

Aquilegia yabeana Kitagawa
in Rep. Exped. Manchukuo 4:81 (1936)

Aquilegia yabeana is another one of those species that get shuffled here and there by taxonomists. Munz considered it a variety of *A. oxysepala*, which will hardly do if *A. oxysepala* is really a variety of *A. buergeriana*. The new *Flora of China* considers both *A. oxysepala* and *A. yabeana* distinct species. Gardeners will hardly care. The plant, a native of central and north-central China (the type locality is Mount Hsia-wu-tai-shan), grows to about 60 cm, with nodding pink-purple flowers, all of one color, on airy stems. The sepals are spreading, oblong, pointed at the tips. The blades are rather short, the spurs are stout and strongly curved. A yellow-flowered form, forma *luteola*, has also been described; this is currently considered not to be distinct from the species itself, except, of course, that the flowers are yellow.

CHAPTER 9

Hybrids and Curiosities

L ONG BEFORE the Sixties and the Summer of Love, columbines were practicing free love. While claims of the astonishing morphological diversity of *Aquilegia* may be exaggerated to some degree, considering the even greater and more astonishing diversity of opinion on the taxonomic identity of a majority of the species, it is true that a large percentage of species with diverse flower shapes are interfertile. Even though some genetic barriers do exist, geographic distribution of the species, including distribution differentiated by elevation, and the means of pollination are the principal barriers to hybridization in the wild. Where species do come in contact, hybridization, usually in the form of hybrid swarms, is relatively common.

In a hybrid swarm, each plant may be slightly different from its neighbor owing to the varying degree of genetic introgression from each species. Studies suggest that the color of the spurs is the feature most likely to be affected by introgression (Hodges and Arnold 1994a). Some individuals within the hybrid swarm may have desirable characteristics from the point of view of horticulture, while others are simply bizarre. Tapping the genetic material of hybrid swarms for new garden plants is something only occasionally practiced; in the genus *Aquilegia*, it is practically never done.

The reason for this is that introgression is a fairly subtle process compared to what may happen in the garden, where geographic barriers completely disappear. In a garden, it is no trouble at all for pollinators to move from a species that they may favor almost exclusively in the wild to another species that they would ordinarily pass by. Whatever inhibitions the species may have had in the wild dissolve into the wildest possible abandon once the plants are introduced to each other. Who knows what debaucheries may go on in nurseries or behind closed garden gates?

And, as we shall see, almost all barriers disappear when breeders work to produce the perfect F_1 hybrid.

Studies of hybridization in *Aquilegia* outnumber taxonomic treatments by a substantial margin, a situation doubtless attributable to the incredible difficulty even of contemplating the taxonomy of the genus, and also to the endless permutations of the genetic material once species are subjected to breeding experiments. While these genetic studies clearly assisted breeders in laying foundations for later work on F_1 hybrids, they also shed new light on the relationships between the species based on genetic characteristics rather than just their appearance and geographical distribution.

Some of the earliest studies showed, or at least attempted to show, that crosses between plants grown from seed obtained from commercial sources (i.e., seed companies or gardens) produced unreliable results owing to the possible "pollution" of the genetic material by other species (Anderson and Schafer 1931). While genetically pure material is theoretically obtainable from garden-grown seed, depending on the time at which the species flowered in the garden and was ready to receive pollinators, acquiring wild-collected seed is essential for the integrity of the experiments. To achieve this, seed would have to be collected from deep within populations of species whose outer distribution range does not come into contact with other species.

Anderson and Schafer crossed at least seven species (*Aquilegia canadensis, A. chrysantha, A. coerulea, A. ecalcarata, A. formosa, A. ×jaeschkanii,* and *A. vulgaris*), as well as "garden varieties of an American long-spurred species" and a garden variety of *A. vulgaris*. The conclusion they drew, after these crosses, was that the resulting hybrids looked more like *A. vulgaris* than they did each other or the parent plants.

This conclusion was taken up by Taylor (1967), who said that many of the hybrids created in experiments in which various species were crossed with other species have the general appearance of *Aquilegia vulgaris*. Nodding flowers, biternate basal leaves, and hooked spurs were shown to be dominant traits inherited by most of the hybrids. Taylor also reported that *A. vulgaris* hybridized readily with all other species in his experiments. He concluded that *A. vulgaris*, not *A. ecalcarata*, must be the ancestral species, the lack of spurs notwithstanding, since *A. vulgaris* also commonly produces spurless plants. Hybrids produced by crossing *A. ecalcarata* with any of the other species in his experiments developed "normal" spurs. It is important to note here that the putative ancestral position of *A. vulgaris* in the genus and the fact that it is the genotype is pure coincidence but a startling one nonetheless—and all because Linnaeus was from Sweden, not California or China.

Taylor's experiments also demonstrated that not all *Aquilegia* species are interfertile. Some of the Asiatic species, *Aquilegia oxysepala* and *A. viridiflora*, for example, seemed completely unwilling to cross with the North American species. All North American species showed a high degree of interfertility among themselves, and most crossed readily with European and most Asian species. The interfertility of the North American species suggested to Taylor that this group of species had evolved more recently than the Old World species. This propensity can have unfortunate results when a mixture of the North American species is grown either in the garden or the nursery.

Since so many of the offspring of various species within *Aquilegia* resemble *Aquilegia vulgaris*, it is often difficult to assign parentage to some of the older hybrids, if that is what they are, and we must rely on the word of earlier garden writers for our information. The close relationship of many species to *A. vulgaris* (*A. olympica*, *A. karelinii*, and so on) and their supposed involvement in some of the hybrids do not help, either.

There is a slight problem with correct identification of many named cultivars. Even these plants—if they are passed down through generations of gardeners who are understandably loath to spend the time necessary to prevent cross-pollination—can lose their original identity. The original characteristics of a cultivar are usually difficult to determine, unless the person who named it is still alive. So many named cultivars and strains have passed out of commerce that they remain just names, and nothing more.

A moderately annoying trend popping up here and there in the nursery trade in the United States is the trademarking of plant names. These trademarked names are then bandied about as cultivar names, but under the 1995 International Code of Nomenclature for Cultivated Plants, cultivar names cannot contain trademarks. In other words, these plants with trademarked names do not have cultivar names. In my opinion, it only adds to the confusion when the same plant is introduced under a genuine cultivar name or turns out to be, as it has in some cases, simply an undescribed species or variety. There may be valid reasons for putting a trademark on plant names, if the intention is to protect the rights of breeders who have put a great deal of time and effort into creating their hybrids; but these plants, in theory at least, also have cultivar names.

The progeny of the horticultural trysts for which the columbine is notorious can be separated into three types. The first are the unintentional hybrids, sometimes of astonishingly little horticultural interest (these would be, no doubt, Parkinson's "degenerate colombines"), but more often than not these children of chance are accidentally wonderful in the garden. The second are the hybrids of commercial horticulture; these may have originally come as surprises to the person in whose garden or nursery they first appeared, but they have been perpetuated by horticulture. The third type are the F_1 hybrids, the products of years of breeding through experiment and careful selection.

The unintentional hybrids, which often masquerade as true species, are a darkly sinister aspect of the wantonness rampant within the genus *Aquilegia*. Only revealing their true parentage when they bloom (if even then), these hybrids, if not discarded by someone familiar with the characteristics of the true species, often pass as the species both in the horticultural trade and from garden to garden. This is certainly the case with a regrettably large number of plants labeled as species in the trade; while these plants are almost always attractive, as I suggested, they do not quite make it for the purist. They also give the wrong impression of the characteristics of the species—impressions that are very difficult to correct once they have been firmly imprinted in the gardener's mind. The state flower of Colorado, where I live, usually turns out to be a hybrid; it might have at least the general appearance of *Aquilegia coerulea*, but it is rarely the right color, as though the original plants dallied in the nursery too long.

Some of these unintentional hybrids have formed the basis upon which named hybrids were created. If a plant has certain desirable characteristics—or the potential for these characteristics is perceived by a keen-eyed gardener—then it may be subjected to further selection and repeatedly crossed with other species or hybrids to produce a stable hybrid, which can then be sent out into the gardening world.

The nature of these interspecific hybrids varies. Some are just seed strains with variable offspring; some are stable hybrids that can be expected to be the same, time and time again.

Aquilegia ×*clematiflora* is a name variously given to plants with nodding, spurless flowers, or sometimes just to plants with spurless flowers. Purists prefer to write the names as cultivars—for example, *A.* 'Clematiflora Alba' (Plate 19) for the plant previously called *A.* ×*clematiflora* 'Alba'. Munz said that, originally, these were spurless forms of the 'Mrs. Scott Elliott' strain, especially in the mauve and pink shades (Plate 18), and occasionally with doubled sepals. The 'Mrs. Scott Elliott' strain, which involves *A. coerulea*, has flowers that can hardly be said to be nodding, so naturally the name has now been appropriated for other cultivars.

The so-called stellate (nodding and spurless) forms of *Aquilegia vulgaris*, ultimately derived from *A. vulgaris* var. *stellata*, have also been called clematiflora types. Part of the confusion here may be the result of the similarity of the word *clematiflora* to the (variously spelled) name once given to these "stellate" forms, *A.* ×*clematiquila*. In any case, the clematiflora name now implies that a more or less nodding spurless flower is to be expected. But, of course, since the lack of spurs is recessive, any plants that cross in the garden or nursery will probably appear with spurs, and another nameless columbine will head down that long road of mystery and confusion.

Aquilegia ×*haenkeana* is so written when this plant is considered a hybrid between *A. vulgaris* and *A. nigricans*; when it was considered by Munz to be nothing more than a synonym of *A. nigricans*, it was written without the ×.

Aquilegia ×*haylodgensis* represented, according to Farrer, a group of hybrids with (possibly) *A. glandulosa* and *A. olympica* as parents; according to Munz these were hybrids involving *A. coerulea*, the other parent, or parents, not being named. The sepals were of practically any color imaginable, the blades yellow, and the spurs "delicate." Various other varieties were at one time available in the trade: var. *delicatissima*, in shades of blue; var. *rosea*, red or pink, sometimes as doubles; and var. *sanguinea*, "sepals dark blood-red, corolla [blades and spurs] soft old-gold" (Munz).

Aquilegia ×*helenae* (also called 'Helenae') is a cross, made around the turn of the last century, between *A. coerulea* and *A. flabellata*. The true plant, which has probably disappeared, was said to be fairly dwarf, with white-tipped blades and fairly long (not short, as is usually suggested) spurs, rather like an *A. flabellata* with the spurs of *A. coerulea*. "The result," Farrer said, "is a really beautiful thing, erect and stiff, about 15 inches [37.5 cm] high, with fine blooms of blue and white, large and firm."

Aquilegia ×*hybrida* (also written as *A. hybrida*) is a name now applied in horticulture to almost any columbine with even the slightest appearance of being a hybrid. In fact the name originally applied to a single cross, putatively of *A. coerulea* and *A. canadensis*, with, according to Munz, pubescent leaves, lilac-purple sepals about 20 mm long, white truncate blades about 10 mm long, blue incurved spurs 20 mm long, and slightly exserted stamens.

Aquilegia ×*jaeschkanii* was supposedly a hybrid between *A. chrysantha* and *A. skinneri*, with red sepals and spurs and yellow blades, "another garden hybrid of no special value," in Farrer's estimation.

Aquilegia ×*oenipontana* is supposedly a naturally occurring hybrid between *A. atrata* and *A. vulgaris*. Munz says the name was proposed "without description," a practice that will be upheld in the present text.

Aquilegia ×*puryearana* is a name given to a relatively recent cross between *A. hinckleyana* and *A. canadensis* that appeared spontaneously in the Navasota, Texas, garden of Pam Puryear. Seeds were then gathered, and the resulting plants were subjected to a ten-year period of selection for best color form. The plants have spreading red sepals, red spurs, and the yellow blades of *A. hinckleyana*, and are said to tolerate the heat and humidity of Texas summers. Plant are sold under the name *A.* ×*puryearana* 'Bernice Ikins', but also under the more generic, and certainly more salable, name of "Blazing Star Columbine." This, a classic case of an unintentional interspecific hybrid brought to stability by concentrated selection, looks like a plant that should be more widely available, and not only in Texas.

Hybrids and Curiosities

Aquilegia ×*stuartii* was a cross of *A. olympica* and *A. glandulosa* that produced a dwarf plant with gigantic flowers (Munz says "up to about 1 dm [10 cm] across"), with flowers the color of *A. glandulosa*, the blades being white-tipped. Farrer despaired of growing it: "It has no constitution at all, wants the coolest and most careful treatment, and often will not respond even to that, and in no case for very long." It is probably no longer in cultivation.

'Hensol Harebell' was a cross between *Aquilegia alpina* and *A. vulgaris* made by Mrs. Kennedy of Castle Douglas in Scotland in the early twentieth century and originally, as Graham Stuart Thomas (1982) says, "of deep Wedgwood blue." Other color variations were raised from seedlings based on this, of various shades, sometimes bicolored; the original hybrid has thus become a strain in which almost anything is possible, but the resulting plants are bound to be much more attractive than their name.

More has been written about 'Hensol Harebell' than perhaps any other interspecific hybrid. Clay (1937) considered it an acceptable substitute for *Aquilegia alpina*; Mansfield (1942) wrote of the "wonderful hybrid of *A. alpina* 'Hensol Harebell' which is a joy in itself." The sepals are somewhat more spreading than typical *A. vulgaris*, and the spurs are hooked, as expected from almost any cross involving *A. vulgaris*. I know this plant only from photographs and can see only a dim semblance of evidence that *A. alpina* was involved in the creation of this famous plant.

The most valuable hybrids, and possibly the most valuable garden plants all in all, are the crosses between two of the most beautiful species, *Aquilegia coerulea* and *A. chrysantha*. Some writers have suggested that *A. formosa* was thrown into the mix to add a red coloration, but no other traits resembling those of *A. formosa* are in evidence in these hybrids. Most of these have the familiar shape and bearing of *A. coerulea* and *A. chrysantha*, but in a wider variety of colors. They have the minor disadvantage of being fairly short-lived and the major desirability of being uniformly beautiful. They are easily raised from seed, and are, of course, readily available almost anywhere plants are sold throughout temperate North America, which is yet another reason for their superiority.

There is much of a muchness about these hybrids; they differ little among themselves except occasionally in height of stem and size of flower. Many of the older hybrid strains, such as the Long-Spurred or

Farquahar Hybrids, are long gone from the trade, replaced by the more stable F₁ hybrids.

A strain can be defined as seed from an original hybrid or group of hybrids (say, in various colors but otherwise having the same habit) that has not been selected for any particular set of characteristics. Seed from the offspring of crosses of *Aquilegia coerulea* and *A. chrysantha* would properly be called a strain. Plants grown from this seed would have certain recognizable characteristics but would potentially be of different colors. The best-known strain of the older series of hybrids is 'Mrs. Scott Elliott,' seed of which is still sometimes available. The strain offers coerulea-chrysantha-type plants with sepals and spurs in various shades from purple to pink to white, with white or off-white blades.

The 'Olympia' strain has plants with long, straight or curving spurs (which ought to assure it is not confused with *Aquilegia olympica*) and offers handsome bicolors with names that give at least some clue as to what colors to expect ('Blue and White', for example). Like the 'Mrs. Scott Elliott' strain, plants come reasonably true from seed.

Members of the 'McKana's Giant' strain (McKana Group; Plate 33), easily the most popular columbines for the garden, are slightly smaller versions (to 80 cm) of the 'Mrs. Scott Elliott' strain, from which they were reputedly derived; again they offer coerulea-chrysantha-type flowers in various shades. A Burpee offering, 'McKana's Giant' won the All-America Selections bronze medal in 1955, and plants are still very much on the market. Dragonfly Hybrids are much the same, but on somewhat shorter stems.

Dwarf Fairyland series, usually offered as a mix, offers plants that are hybrids, possibly of *Aquilegia vulgaris* and others, with pink, rose, or red upward-facing flowers on 20 cm stems. The flowers are single or double, the petals rather tubular, with short spurs. Except for the leaves, plants have little in common with ordinary columbines. I prefer not to comment on the effect these flowers have on me; Graham Stuart Thomas's characterization of them as an "abomination" is the way they strike some gardeners (Thomas 1982). Their dwarf characteristic has, however, played a major role in other breeding programs.

'Biedermeier' is another dwarf strain, almost always sold as a mix of colors (white, rose, and purple). The occasional attribution of these plants to *Aquilegia sibirica* is incomprehensible to me.

The F_1 hybrids are different. While the term F_1 (first filial generation) hybrid is applied, generally, to the offspring of a cross between two species, here it is used with strict intent: namely, to identify the offspring of two parents inbred solely for the purpose of creating a race of plants with stable, definable characteristics. In other words, each potential parent is subject to rigorous inbreeding until the desired elements are obtained, and then the two parents are crossed to provide seed. Inbreeding of parents may take several generations before each parent has been bred for ideal qualities. Plants obtained from this seed often show characteristics superior to either parent, a phenomenon known as heterosis, or "hybrid vigor." Careful selection results in an accumulation of dominant genes with favorable characteristics (disease resistance being an obvious example). The line of each parent must be maintained, of course, in order to produce seed every year.

A recognizable name associated with these F_1 hybrids is important both to the gardener, for whom the name means proven performance and stability, and to the breeder, who is then able to keep the line going and have their name attached to the hybrids. Here is where trademarked names are justified; for one thing, it keeps inferior plants from being sold under the trademarked name.

The Music (or Musik) and Dynasty series offer several colors, usually with names like 'Blue and White' or 'Pink and White'. Similar to 'McKana's Giant', these grow to about 60 cm. But probably the most notable F_1 hybrid columbines are those of the Songbird series. These plants were the creation of the late Charles L. Weddle, Jr., of Paonia, Colorado, who was, according to John White, one of the premier plant breeders of the twentieth century. (Music and Dynasty series are also his creations, and quite similar.) Weddle crossed *Aquilegia coerulea* with the 'McKana's Giant' strain and the Dwarf Fairyland series to create the Songbird series; these columbines come in different heights and have slightly different applications in the garden. They are especially favored by commercial growers, who are able to produce flowering-sized plants in one season if the seed is sown in early winter.

Songbird series plants are often available in garden centers, at least in this country. They are also available as seed strains. All are extremely beautiful and well worth acquiring. 'Blue Jay' is dark blue and white, and grows to 75 cm. 'Blue Bird' is light blue and white, grows to 60 cm, and is especially recommended for nurseries since it shows considerable vigor in the cell packs, often growing more robustly than the other varieties in spring (Nau 1996). 'Dove' has white flowers and grows to 60 cm; 'Goldfinch' (Plate 4) is pale yellow and grows to the same height, as does 'Robin', which has pale pink sepals and white blades. The taller varieties are also recommended for cut flowers. 'Cardinal' grows to 45 cm and has deep red sepals and white blades. 'Bunting' (Plate 14) is essentially the same as 'Blue Bird' but grows to 50 cm and is often recommended for the rock garden.

Another name that has flitted past my consciousness at least once, 'Tanager', seems to be out of commerce. I have never seen this plant, but since tanagers here have yellow bodies, black wings, and red heads, I can only wonder what this plant must have looked like.

Sources of Seed

❦

A LARGE SELECTION of seed, mostly garden-grown, is available from the major rock garden societies. Yearly seed lists are sent to active members; contact each group for current membership rates.

As of this writing, regulations may make it difficult for U.S. citizens to obtain seed from overseas; bureaucracies being what they are, this may even include seed of columbines native to the United States, raised in other countries.

The North American Rock Garden Society
Executive Secretary
P.O. Box 67
Millwood, NY 10546
www.nargs.org

The Alpine Garden Society
AGS Centre
Avon Bank, Pershore, Worcs. WR10 3JP
U.K.
www.alpinegardensociety.org/index2.html

4

The Scottish Rock Garden Club
Subscription Secretary
Mrs. Hazel Smith
c/o Harrylayock, Solsgirth
Dollar FK14 7NE
U.K.
www.srgc.org.uk

Wild-collected seed is also available. A number of people offer seed collected on various expeditions; the selection is often not large, but the species may be ones rarely seen in cultivation. There are two major sources for wild-collected columbine seed, both in North America:

Northwest Native Seed
17595 Vierra Canyon Rd. #172
Prunedale, CA 93907
$2 for catalog

Southwestern Native Seeds
P.O. Box 50503
Tucson, AZ 85703
$2 for catalog

Glossary

biternate. Doubly ternate.

blade. The lower part of the petal; the inside five-parted section of the *Aquilegia* flower.

cauline. On the stem.

cespitose. Tufted.

concolorous. All one color. In *Aquilegia* (or at least in this book), the greenish tint at the tips of the sepals is occasionally ignored when describing flowers as concolorous.

divergent. Held at a slight angle away from an axis; in *Aquilegia*, used to describe the position of the sepals with reference to an axis drawn in a line created by the flower stalk (pedicel) through the center of the flower.

endemic. Confined to one particular region, soil type, etc.

equal. As long as (or as short as).

exserted. Protruding beyond; in *Aquilegia*, refers to the position of the staminodes relative to the end of the blades.

follicle. A dehiscent (splitting-open) fruit opening on one side.

glabrous. Smooth; hairless.

glandular. Having glands; usually sticky to the touch.

glaucous. Covered with bloom, as in grapes; a waxy appearance.

included. Remaining within the corolla; not exserted. Refers to stamens or staminodes.

inflorescence. The flowering stalk.

Isopyrum. A genus in the Ranunculaceae (Linnaeus, Sp. Pl. 557, 1753) of about thirty species with biternate basal leaves, small white flowers with short-tubular or sac-like petals (instead of spurs), no staminodes, and smooth seeds.

lamina (plural **laminae**). The blade.

limb. The lobes of the corolla, taken in entirety.

petal. The inner part of the flower; in *Aquilegia*, the blade and spur together. Sometimes called a honey-leaf in the context of this genus.

pilose. Covered with long, soft hairs.

pubescent. Covered with short, soft hairs, or, generally, hairy.

saccate. Pouch-like; in *Aquilegia*, refers to undeveloped spurs.

sepal. A leaf-like segment of the calyx; in *Aquilegia*, the outside of the flower, five-parted; the "doves." Called petals in some treatments. Sometimes correctly pronounced with a short e, as in petal.

spreading. Giving the appearance of being spread open; refers to the sepals.

spur. The narrow, sometimes hooked, nectar-bearing upper portion of the petal.

stamen. The male organ of a flower.

staminode. A sterile stamen.

suberect. Not fully upright, but more upright than nodding.

ternate. In threes.

triternate. Triply ternate.

type. The variety with characters most essential to the species; the type species is the species itself, without the qualifications of varieties or forms. The type locality is the place where the species or variety was originally found. Up until about 1880 this location could be as vague as a gesture in the general direction of a continent; currently, it is expected to be as precise as possible. The intent is that the scientifically curious, or the lover of wildflowers, may go to the described location and find the plant described.

Urophysa. A genus in the Ranunculaceae (Ulbrich, Notizbl. Bot. Gart. Berlin-Dahlem 10:868, 1929) of two species with sepals and petals of roughly the same size and palmate trifoliate basal leaves. The petals have short or saccate spurs; there are five to ten staminodes; the seeds are wrinkled. With *Isopyrum*, sometime home of many species of *Aquilegia* and *Semiaquilegia*.

villous. Closely covered with long, soft hairs. Denser than pilose.

viscid. Sticky.

Bibliography

Anderson, Edgar, and Brenhilda Schafer. 1931. Species hybrids in *Aquilegia. Annals of Botany* 45(180):639–646.

Barr, Claude A. 1983. *Jewels of the Plains: Wildflowers of the Great Plains Grasslands and Hills.* Minneapolis: University of Minnesota Press.

Bulavkina, A. A. 1937. "*Aquilegia.*" In *Flora of the U.S.S.R.* Jerusalem: Israel Program for Scientific Translation.

Chowdhery, H. J., and B. M. Wadhwa. 1984. *Flora of Himachal Pradesh.* New Delhi: Botanical Survey of India.

Clay, Sampson. 1937. *The Present-Day Rock Garden.* London: T. C. & E. C. Jack.

Copeland, Linda L., and Allan M. Armitage. 2001. *Legends in the Garden.* Atlanta, Ga.: Green Leaves Press. Distributed by Timber Press, Portland, Ore.

Correll, Donovan S., and Marshall C. Johnston. 1970. *Manual of the Vascular Plants of Texas.* Renner, Tex.: Texas Research Foundation.

Correvon, Henri, and Philippe Robert. [1911]. *The Alpine Flora.* London: Methuen & Co.

Cullen, J., V. H. Heywood, and J. R. Akeroyd. 1993. "*Aquilegia.*" In *Flora Europaea.* 2nd ed., edited by T. G. Tutin et al. Cambridge: Cambridge University Press.

Damboldt, J., and W. Zimmermann. 1965. "*Aquilegia.*" In *Illustrierte Flora von Mittel-Europa.* 2nd ed. Orig. ed. edited by Gustav Hegi. Berlin: Verlag Paul Parey.

Davis, Ray J. 1952. *Flora of Idaho*. Provo, Utah: Brigham Young University Press.

Davis, T. D., D. Sankhla, N. Sankhla, A. Upadhyaya, J. M. Parsons, and S. W. George. 1993. Improving seed germination of *Aquilegia chrysantha* by temperature manipulation. *HortScience* 28(8):798–799.

DeSanto, Jerry. 1991. Variations in *Aquilegia jonesii*. *Bulletin of the American Rock Garden Society* 49(1):60–65.

Dezhi, Fu, and Orbélia R. Robinson. 2001. "*Aquilegia*." In *Flora of China*. Online document.

Diaz Gonzáles, T. E. 1986. "*Aquilegia*." In *Flora Iberica*, edited by Castroviejo et al. Madrid: Real Jardín Botánico, C.S.I.C.

Dorn, Robert D. 1988. *Vascular Plants of Wyoming*. Cheyenne, Wyo.: Mountain West Publishing.

Drummond, J. R., and J. Hutchinson. 1920. A revision of *Isopyrum* (Ranunculaceae) and its nearer allies. *Kew Bulletin of Miscellaneous Information* 1920:145–169.

Farrer, Reginald. 1907. *My Rock-Garden*. London: Edwin Arnold.

———. 1919. *The English Rock-Garden*. Edinburgh: T.C. and E. C. Jack.

Gleason, Henry A., and Arthur Cronquist. 1991. 2nd ed. *Manual of Vascular Plants of Northeastern United States and Adjacent Canada*. Bronx: The New York Botanical Garden.

Grant, Verne. 1952. Isolation and hybridization between *Aquilegia formosa* and *A. pubescens*. *El Aliso* 2(4):341–360.

Hickman, James C., ed. 1993. *The Jepson Manual: Higher Plants of California*. Berkeley and Los Angeles: University of California Press.

Hitchcock, C. Leo, and Arthur Cronquist. 1973. *Flora of the Pacific Northwest*. Seattle: University of Washington Press.

Hodges, Scott A. 1997a. Flora nectar spurs and diversification. *International Journal of Plant Sciences* 158 (6 Suppl.):S81–S88.

———. 1997b. "Rapid Radiation Due to a Key Innovation in Columbines (Ranunculaceae: *Aquilegia*)." In *Molecular Evolution and Adaptive Radiation*, edited by Thomas J. Givnish and Kenneth J. Sytsma. Cambridge: Cambridge University Press.

Hodges, Scott A., and Michael L. Arnold. 1994a. Floral and ecological isolation between *Aquilegia formosa* and *Aquilegia pubescens*. *Proceedings of the National Academy of Sciences USA* 91:2493–2496.

————. 1994b. Columbines: a geographically widespread species flock. *Proceedings of the National Academy of Sciences USA* 91:5129–5132.

————. 1995. Spurring plant diversification: are floral nectar spurs a key innovation? *Proceedings of the Royal Society of London* 262:343–348.

Kearney, Thomas H., and Robert H. Peebles. 1951. *Arizona Flora.* Berkeley: University of California Press.

Lancaster, Roy. 1993. *Travels in China: A Plantsman's Paradise.* Woodbridge, U.K.: Antique Collector's Club.

Lott, Emily. 1985. New combinations in Chihuahuan Desert *Aquilegia* (Ranunculaceae). *Phytologia* 58(7):488.

Lloyd, Christopher. 2000. *Christopher Lloyd's Garden Flowers.* Portland, Ore.: Timber Press.

Mansfield, T. C. 1942. *Alpines in Colour and Cultivation.* London: Britain in Pictures (Publishers) Limited.

Mengel, Lisa Ann. 1981. "Effects of Irradiance and Photoperiod on Growth and Flowering of Selected Herbaceous Perennials." Master's thesis, Pennsylvania State University.

Miller, Russell B. 1981. Hawkmoths and the geographical patterns of floral variation in *Aquilegia caerulea. Evolution* 35(4):763–774.

————. 1985. Hawkmoth pollination of *Aquilegia chrysantha* (Ranunculaceae) in southern Arizona. *The Southwestern Naturalist* 30(1):69–76.

Moerman, Daniel E. 1998. *Native American Ethnobotany.* Portland, Ore.: Timber Press.

Munz, Philip A. 1946. The cultivated and wild columbines. *Gentes Herbarum* 7:1–150.

Munz, Philip A., and David D. Keck. 1959. *A California Flora.* Berkeley and Los Angeles: University of California Press.

Nau, Jim. 1996. *Ball Perennial Manual: Propagation and Production.* Batavia, Ill.: Ball Publishing.

Ohwi, Jisaburo. 1965. "*Aquilegia.*" In *Flora of Japan*, edited by Frederick G. Meyer and Egbert H. Wakert. Washington, D.C.: Smithsonian Institution.

Payson, Edwin Blake. 1918. The North American species of *Aquilegia. Contributions from the U.S. National Herbarium* 20:133–157.

Perry, L. P. 1995. 'Corbett' columbine. *HortScience* 30(1):165.

Phillips, Roger, and Martyn Rix. 1992. *Early Perennials.* Vol. 1 of *The Random House Book Perennials.* New York: Random House.

Pignatti, Sandro. 1982. *Flora d'Italia.* Bologna: Edagricole.

Polunin, Oleg. 1980. *Flowers of Greece and the Balkans.* Oxford: Oxford University Press.

Polunin, Oleg, and Adam Stainton. 1997. *Flowers of the Himalayas.* Delhi: Oxford University Press.

Prażmo, W. 1965. Cytogenetic studies on the genus *Aquilegia. Acta Societatis Botanicorum Poloniae* 34(3):403–437.

Proctor, Michael, Peter Yeo, and Andrew Lack. 1996. *The Natural History of Pollination.* Portland, Ore.: Timber Press.

Rechinger, Karl Heinz. 1992. *Flora Iranica.* Graz: Akademische Druck und Verlagsanstalt.

Robinson, William. 1900. *The English Flower Garden and Home Grounds.* 8th ed. London: John Murray.

Rowntree, Lester. 1936. *Hardy Californians.* New York: The Macmillan Co.

Schafer, Brenhilda. 1941. The genetics of *Aquilegia vulgaris. Journal of Genetics* 41:339–347.

Schenk, George. 1984. *The Complete Shade Gardener.* Boston: Houghton Mifflin. Reprinted with emendations in 2002 by Timber Press, Portland, Ore.

Shipchinskii, N. V. 1937. "*Semiaquilegia* and *Paraquilegia.*" In *Flora of the U.S.S.R.* Jerusalem: Israel Program for Scientific Translation.

Strid, Arne. 1986. *Mountain Flowers of Greece.* Cambridge: Cambridge University Press.

Taylor, Ronald J. 1967. Interspecific hybridization and its evolutionary significance in the genus *Aquilegia. Brittonia* 19:374–390.

Taylor, Ronald J., and David Campbell. 1969. Biochemical systematics and phylogenetic interpretations in the genus *Aquilegia. Evolution* 23:153–162.

Thomas, Graham Stuart. 1982. *Perennial Garden Plants.* 2nd ed. London: J. M. Dent and Sons.

Walters, S. M., et al. 1989. *The European Garden Flora.* Cambridge: Cambridge University Press.

Weber, William A. 1987. *Colorado Flora: Western Slope.* Boulder, Colo.: Colorado Associated University Press.

Welsh, Stanley L., N. Duane Atwood, Sherel Goodrich, and Larry C. Higgins. 1987. *A Utah Flora*. Provo, Utah: Brigham Young University.

Whittemore, Alan T. 1997. "*Aquilegia*." In *Flora of North America*, edited by Nancy R. Morin. New York: Oxford University Press.

Wooton, E. O., and Paul C. Standley. 1915. *Flora of New Mexico: Contributions from the U.S. National Herbarium*. Washington, D.C.: Government Printing Office.

Zhang, Xuri. 1987. "Regulation of Flowering in *Aquilegia*." Master's thesis, Pennsylvania State University.

Index

Italicized page numbers refer to illustrations in the text.